To President George W. Bush

Warrior-Statesman

I will not forget this wound to our country or those who inflicted it. I will not yield; I will not rest; I will not relent in waging this struggle for freedom and security for the American people.

WAR

From the Caves to the Towers to Hell

Dr. Mike Stoddard
Visiting Fellow, The Oxford Institute on Institutional Law & Justice
Academic Dean, The Oxford Study Abroad Programme
Lecturer, San Diego State University

With the Special Assistance of:
Professor Don McCann
and
Michael McCann, JD, Deputy District Attorney

© 2007 Dr. Mike Stoddard
www.docstoddard.com

© 2007 KB Books
info@kbbooks.com
www.kbbooks.com

All Rights reserved, no part of this publication may be reproduced, stored in a retrieval system, or transmitted, in any form or by any means, electronic, mechanical, photocopying, recording, or otherwise, without the prior written permission from the publisher or the author.

ISBN 0-9717216-0-2

2007 Oxford Edition

All copyrighted material in this document has been obtained with permission from the copyright holder and appropriate recognitions have been made.

Executive Editor: Shane Coons
Editorial Assistant: Andrew Shorb
Developmental Editor: Donald McCann, Jr.
Technical Editor: Robert Brown

TABLE OF CONTENTS

Part I The War on Terrorism

Preface	7
Introduction	10
What Has Happened	12
America Lashes Back	18
What Caused It	20
The Call To Arms	23
Armageddon Revisited	25

Part II Two Balances of Power

Balance Number 1	30
Balance Number 2	38

Part III Operation Iraqi Freedom

The Winds Of War	44
Prelude To War	53
Campaign Iraq	57

Part IV Conclusion

Lessons From The Past	69
Realpolitik Revisited	74
What Will Be Next	76
Epilogue	81
Lecture – Oxford University	81
E Mail Note	83

Part V Country Profiles

Afghanistan	87
Bahrain	92
Egypt	96
Iran	101

Iraq	106
Israel	112
Jordan	118
Kuwait	123
Pakistan	127
Saudi Arabia	133
Somalia	138
Sudan	142
Syria	147
Tajikistan	151
Turkey	155
Turkmenistan	160
United Arab Emirates	164
Uzbekistan	169

Appendixes

A Terrorist Organizations	173
B Battle Map	176
C Military Strength Comparisons	177
D The Academy And The Sea	179
E Remarks/President Bush	186
F September 20, 2001 Address On Terrorism	187
G Address/USS Abraham Lincoln	195
H Prime Minister Blair's Address to Congress	200
I President Bush Discusses Freedom in Iraq And Middle East	212
J President Bush's Inaugural Address 2005	221
K President's Address to the Nation December 18, 2005	226

PREFACE

Although this short book was put together rather quickly because of the rush of events, I hope it will prove to be useful to students interested in and worried about the War on Terrorism. The War on Terrorism is particularly disturbing to Americans because their homeland is involved, but it is in a strange kind of way also totally exhilarating. Rarely has the American nation moved so quickly and with so much unity toward a political objective. Rarely has a new era of international politics been introduced so obviously and clearly. My parents' generation dealt with the horrors of National Socialism and Fascism. My generation lived with the nightmare of what President Reagan correctly called the "evil empire" and the worldwide communist movement that at one point controlled one half of the people of the earth.

I am firmly convinced that President George W. Bush is correct—the American generation of today will be called upon to save their nation, their way of life, and their civilization. Their moment has arrived; their rendezvous with destiny is at hand. I have instructed young people all of my adult life. I am confident I am an expert on really nothing at all—but I do know one thing positively—this generation will meet the call, they will make us proud, and when the darkness passes we will be astounded by our children of light.

I would like to dedicate this presentation and all of the classes I have taught to my two godsons, Mike McCann and Donald McCann, Jr., who have brought me unending pleasure and who have made an otherwise confusing existence completely clear. They dazzle all who meet them with their charm, civility, good cheer, and intelligence. My most fervent prayer is that I shall be allowed to watch, with what I know will be total satisfaction and pride, as their wonderful lives progress.

I owe a special debt of gratitude to Professor Don McCann who currently teaches for the United States Navy. Don has been a friend for more than 30 years. His organizational and intellectual talents are really quite extraordinary. He worked feverishly on this project as he has on all my projects blindly assuming it might prove to be of some value to our students.

I would like also to offer special thanks to Professor Robert Scheuttinger, Director of the Oxford Study Abroad Programme. Bob is a brilliant academic and a wonderful friend. He has made it possible for hundreds of my students to study with programmes affiliated with Oxford University. Andrew Shorb must also be mentioned. Andrew has been my academic and administrative assistant for several years both in San Diego and in Oxford. He is a magnificent young academic with a most promising future. He has also become a wonderful friend.

It is impossible to list all of the student/friends I have known, respected, and enjoyed over the years. Suffice it to say that they have allowed me to have a magnificent life and it may be a mark of their talents that I can now say with absolute confidence, if I could live my life over again I would change nothing and I would trade with no one.

Dr. Mike Stoddard
San Diego, California
January 2007

PART I
THE WAR ON TERRORISM

INTRODUCTION

Sept. 11, 2001 is a date most Americans will know about to the end of time. Although the United States has endured horribly difficult times in the past, most notably the Civil War and World War II, never has the nation been so shattered and shocked by a single day in its history. Pearl Harbor comes to mind but Dec. 7, 1941 involved a foreign empire and an attack on the US military. Sept. 11 involved an attack on innocent civilians—an attack from a mysterious, dark force.

The purpose of this presentation is to provide students of government with a fairly brief, inexpensive set of notes and essays designed to make the maddeningly complicated War on Terrorism more understandable. The study of politics is about power and the ability to control and influence people and nations. It is, however, a process, which by its very nature is imprecise, baffling, and confusing. We are able to predict political events only very superficially. We will in all likelihood never have much precision in our discipline. We can, nevertheless, be quite sophisticated about how little we know. In times of crisis, especially of the kind confronting the nation today, it becomes essential to bring forth our greatest talents—a great deal is at stake—the lives of our soldiers, the lives of Americans at home, the destiny of freedom everywhere, indeed perhaps the future of Western Civilization itself.

The study of international politics is more than anything else the study of violence and war. Man has never and no doubt will never achieve schemes of government, which are able to bring order and civility to the international system. Considering the fact that the first priority of all governments is to maintain order, it is quite frightening to contemplate the level of power an international authority would have to reach in order to maintain order throughout the world. The international system can, nevertheless, develop enough order to deal with some threats. Global terrorism is that kind of threat. The 40 nation Coalition patched together by President George W. Bush after Sept. 11 may well be the beginning.

It will no doubt be a revolving Coalition with varying levels of support. It will no doubt have members join and drop out unexpectedly but it may very well hold enough of the people of the world together to substantially alter international politics—to substantially alter the pattern of global terrorism. The inviolate nature of national sovereignty is at stake—it is most surprising, perhaps amazing that an American President could so quickly mobilize international support for what has come to be known of as the Bush Doctrine—the idea that those nations which host terrorists are in fact terrorists themselves.

The War on Terrorism like all wars ultimately will involve a struggle about ideas, values, civilizations, and ideologies. It may in the end be vital that America for 230 years has been one of the few beacons of hope in a world racked with famine, war and slavery. The Americans are particularly interesting because they are free and because they trace their ancestry to all parts of the planet. The expression E Pluribus Unum which is found on all American coins means "from many, one"—from many races, religions, ethnic groups, civilizations—one, the Americans. This grand experiment in politics may be exactly suited to lead the races, religions, ethnic groups, and civilizations of the world in the destruction of terrorism, which preys on the weak and defenseless.

American politics and American political institutions are about limiting power—limiting power so that men and women can be free. The Americans have operationalized their version of freedom with several doctrines—the doctrine of the separation of powers which calls for an independent Congress, President and High Court; the doctrine of the division of power which outlines the division of power between the central government and the states; and the doctrine of judicial review which provides the Supreme Court with the power to rule on the constitutionality of law.

The American political system has limited power with remarkable success. If the founders and particularly the authors of the Federalist Papers were to return for a visit they would no doubt be astounded by how faithfully their scheme has been followed. The fact that this scheme works quite oddly, slowly, and inefficiently seems to bother the Americans not at all.

The American system however is remarkably deceiving. When a national crisis confronts the nation, a political system characterized by inefficiency and bickering can quickly become an engine of monumental power and efficiency. Abraham Lincoln and Franklin Delano Roosevelt rearranged American political institutions to the point that they ruled nearly as "constitutional dictators." Within the constitutional structure, they rallied the nation to its most important victories. President Bush and his successors may not have to adopt such extraordinary powers, but if they do, and if the public and the political establishment support them, they will find little in the US political structure that will hinder them. The nation's capacity to move decisively and swiftly was clearly demonstrated by the extraordinary and brilliant campaigns carried out in Afghanistan in 2001 and Iraq in 2003.

The War on Terrorism as British Prime Minister Blair has noted is "clearly, plainly a war about freedom and civilization." Most men for most of history have wanted to be free, to live in peace, and to attain some prosperity. Perhaps it is possible that America will use its current dominion in this second of history, to advance all three. If we are to have a special destiny—if President Bush is correct, "that our moment has arrived," and we are to succeed, it will surely involve abandoning forever the "natural" American tendency to hide on our island surrounded by wonderful neighbors and safe oceans and "let the rest of the world go by." Perhaps we should add to our currency: "if you do not know where you are going, any road will take you there." The Americans used their staggering power to destroy Fascism and Communism—perhaps now they will lead the world to the destruction of global terrorism and its handmaidens—famine and tyranny.

WHAT HAS HAPPENED

On Sept. 11, 2001, the United States homeland was struck by four jumbo jets hitting the New York Trade Center and the Pentagon. The "kamikaze" type assault was immediately labeled by President George W. Bush as an act of war. The next day the Congress joined the President in using similar language in a Resolution of Congress passed nearly unanimously by both houses. The attack was particularly shocking and particularly lethal.

The United States had lost large numbers of its citizens on a single day in the past—at Iwo Jima, Gettysburg, D-Day, and Pearl Harbor—but never had the American homeland been struck so violently and so fatally for thousands of civilians. The final terrible tally may never be known but something in the range of 3000 civilians were killed in New York and Washington, D.C. and something in the range of another 6,000 were seriously injured.

The scheme of the terrorists may also never be known but at the most general level their overall strategy seems clear—to attack as ferociously as possible the political, military, and economic centers of the United States. The New York Trade Center was a perfect target to demonstrate the vulnerable nature of America's extraordinary but highly synchronized economy as well as the world's economic dependence on the

United States. The Pentagon is obviously the center of America's military empire. The fourth jet, which missed its target, was probably en route to the US Capitol or the White House, clearly the centers of the American political system. It is also noteworthy that citizens of 86 other countries died in the attack with the United Kingdom having the greatest losses—something in the range of 300.

Although the emotional part of the tragedy involving so much human death and misery overwhelmed the press and the public, some calculation of the economic costs of the attack is in order. Mayor Guliani of New York estimated that the structural damage to the New York Trade Center and adjacent buildings was in the range of $20 billion and full restoration would be in the range of $40 billion. Also, the New York Stock exchange was closed for nearly a week with a somewhat incalculable hit on the economy. Once the market opened five days after the attack, the Dow Jones average dropped in a free fall kind of way losing 14 percent of its value in five days, marking the worst single week in the stock exchanges' long history. Air travel throughout the nation was severely reduced and the airlines faced economic ruin. More than 100,000 airline employees lost their jobs within 10 days of the attack. Auto sales dropped by 25 percent from Sept. 11 to Oct. 1 indicating the American economy, which was in some difficulty before Sept. 11, was clearly headed for recession.

There are four parts to the colossal American economy—consumer spending, capital investment, exports, and government spending. The first three declined dramatically after Sept. 11. The fourth increased at the federal level but that represents only a small part of the nation's overall economic activity. Moreover, federal spending increases on defense and homeland security were more than offset by declines in state and local government spending. State and local governments must balance their budgets and of course do not have the luxury of printing money.

The terrorists drastically harmed all four general aspects of the American economy. There is an old saying that will no doubt be true again—those who bet against the American economy will lose, but in the "short" run America was headed for what appeared to be a deep and difficult recession. It became clear early on that the War on Terrorism would be fought on three fronts—overseas, the homeland, and the economy. The economy would need good news from the other two fronts in order to begin the recovery. The recovery would come—the unsettling question of course was "when." Importantly, by the end of 2001, the military situation in Afghanistan was such that the Dow Jones average soared to 10,000. With US interest rates at a 20 year low and consumer spending beginning to rally, 2002 had all of the trappings of a major recovery. However, war in Iraq in 2003 brought more uncertainty and sluggishness to the economy. The volatile nature of the economy and the intimate relationship between the War and the US economy was revealed again in 2007 as the nation experienced surprising levels of economic growth. Rather amazingly the New Stock Exchange reached a new historic high.

At some point in the calmer future it may be possible to evaluate all of the economic costs of having massive disruptions to the transportation, communication, and military systems of the United States. It is noteworthy that the Congress authorized $40 billion in immediate emergency aid with an additional $100 billion marked for supplemental DOD spending. The Congress and the White House were in agreement that the Pentagon's budget would be more than doubled in the very near future. The President asked for and received nearly $400 billion for the Department of Defense in his budget request for 2003 with an additional $38 billion earmarked for homeland security and another $40 billion for Operation Iraqi Freedom. In 2004, the President asked for and Congress authorized $87 billion for the reconstruction of Iraq. Total spending for defense and homeland security exceeded $500 billion in 2007. In the end, it will no doubt be clear that the United States lost hundreds of billions of dollars leaving aside the costs of financing the reconstruction that followed. September 11th probably cost the West close to $1 trillion. All that is clear now is that the United States and the Western world cannot sustain such economic hits often and maintain their economic well-being.

The human carnage related to the attack is impossible to calculate. Suffice it to say that the nation suffered even more horror than the casualties themselves. Although rage, demands for retribution, calls for an American Jihad, remarkable outbursts of patriotism and public service filled the air it was also clear that a certain national malaise had set in. Largely undiscussed fear was present in all corners. Children asked questions about their security and their nation rarely heard in the United States. University students inquired about conscription and wondered about their futures. Reports following the attack of threats to the national water supply system, train system, trucking system, and nuclear plants added a whole new dimension to the problem. Attorney General Ashcroft reported the possibility of crop dusting planes being used in a chemical attack on US cities. Additionally, he warned our European Allies that similar attacks might be planned for them. Director of the CIA, George Tenet, warned that important national events such as the Olympics and Joint Sessions of Congress would be on the terrorists' "hit list" indefinitely.

On Oct. 12, 2001 the War took a new, curious, frightening twist. A media group corporation in Florida reported that anthrax had been discovered in its mailroom. The anthrax infected two employees one of whom died. The FBI and medical teams swarmed into Florida to contain the situation. Two days later Tom Brokaw's office in New York received a letter covered with finely ground anthrax. One of Brokaw's assistants was diagnosed as having the anthrax infection on her skin. Two days later on Oct. 16 a letter containing more anthrax appeared in the Senate Majority Leader's office. The Capitol was evacuated; the House of Representatives was closed for five days, 31 congressional staff people tested positive for anthrax. Curiously the Senate, where the anthrax was found, stayed in session. Clearly the Congress was adjusting, with some confusion, to a world with which it had little experience. It was perhaps a hallmark of America's new situation that the US Congress had not been closed because of outside events since the British invasion of 1812. Shortly after the Capitol scare several postal workers tested positive for anthrax. Two died. It was particularly disturbing to the nation that its postal service of 600,000 employees who manage more than 600,000,000 pieces of mail per day had become part of the front-line of war.

It was unclear whether or not the anthrax attacks on Florida, New York, and Washington, D.C. were part of a foreign terrorist attack but it seemed safe to assume that there was some connection. The nation responded with great concern but little panic. Perhaps most chilling was not the anthrax itself but rather the fact that America would now have to prepare its homeland defense for continuing biochemical attacks. On Oct. 18 the new Director of Homeland Defense, Former Governor Tom Ridge of Pennsylvania, announced that the US would begin stockpiling the appropriate amounts of small pox vaccine, penicillin, cero and other medical agents, which might be needed in a world of bioterrorism. The President's chilling warnings from Sept. 11 on defined the battle. America was indeed at war and the homeland for the first time in American history would be under continuing assault.

More positively, several rather astounding political developments occurred shortly after Sept. 11. The European Union, still largely an economic union, passed unanimously with all 15 members an unprecedented political resolution offering unqualified and unlimited assistance as well as condolences to the American people. America's primary military alliance, NATO, with all 19 members concurring invoked

Article 5 for the first time in its 53-year history. Article 5 states that an "attack upon one NATO country will be regarded as an attack upon them all." Article 5 has always been understood to involve a Soviet or Russian attack on Western Europe which would bring America to Europe's defense. It was astounding and reassuring to Americans that NATO seemed in this unexpected way to be returning a favor accumulated over 53 years of enjoying the American shield.

The United Nations Security Council, with all 15 members voting unanimously, supported an American resolution against terrorism. The Security Council invoked Chapter 5 of the UN charter demanding that all 192 nations move immediately to stop the training, movement, and financing of international terrorism. The Organization of American states adopted a similar resolution. Perhaps in the end even more importantly, virtually all of America's Arab and Muslim Allies rallied to the cause. All withdrew recognition from the Taliban—the illegitimate government of Afghanistan, which had so long harbored and encouraged terrorists. The Gulf States, Saudi Arabia, Jordan, Egypt, Pakistan, Turkey, Indonesia and others joined the emerging American led Coalition. Within a few days of the assault on America, at least publicly, Afghanistan and the world of terrorism stood alone with the exception of Iraq. China and Russia joined the Coalition. Perhaps most shocking, three former Soviet Republics, Turkmenistan, Uzbekistan, and Tajikistan all agreed to open their airspace and provide other forms of assistance to the United States military. Russia itself authorized an air corridor for US aircraft in need of help or for those involved in humanitarian relief.

Militarily, America began almost immediately to move. Five aircraft carriers were dispatched to the Arabian Sea, the Arabian Gulf, and the Mediterranean. Three hundred warplanes in addition to the aircraft on the carriers were sent to the Middle Eastern theatre. Special Forces, particularly the 82nd Airborne division from North Carolina, the Mountain Division from Maine, and the 101st Airborne division from Kentucky were put on the highest alert. By the second week it was clear that American and British Special Forces were on the ground in Afghanistan preparing the way for a larger assault.

The air campaign started on Oct. 6. Within two weeks the US had dropped 2000 precision-guided bombs on Afghan targets. The Taliban was clearly on the run. The Northern Alliance was poised to take control of the entire northern part of Afghanistan and move toward Kabul. The first wave of the air campaign involved destroying military installations, command and control centers, and all air defense systems. This mission was accomplished within 12 days. The second wave of the air campaign moved toward "targets of opportunity" meaning soldiers, trucks, and tanks on the move. US C130 aircraft and helicopters were used in the attacks. Total air supremacy was established as well as the ability to support Northern Alliance, US Special Forces, and other Coalition forces on the ground. The air campaign followed the same pattern that had been employed in Desert Storm in 1991 and Kosovo in 1999—air supremacy first, ground activity second. The nature of the air campaign was extraordinary and one would imagine staggering to the enemy. US field commanders indicated they were running out of targets while using less than 20 percent of their firepower.

The US criminal justice system moved into the crisis in an unprecedented way. More than 7000 FBI agents and 4000 staff began tracking down nearly 200,000 leads. Hundreds were detained and America's Allies detained scores more as arrests were made throughout the US and Europe. The web of horror with its incredibly obvious paper trail began to unwind. In addition, 40 nations joined the US in attempting to block terrorist financial resources. Attempts of this kind had been made before but never so elaborately and never so completely. Perhaps the greatest economic hammer was the President's order that financial institutions doing business with terrorists would be banned from all US markets.

One of the most extraordinary developments of the crisis was political in nature. The Congress, indeed the entire American political establishment, rallied to the nation in a way not seen since World War II. As would be expected, the American President became the focal point of national attention. George W. Bush's approval rating went from 60 percent a few days before Sept. 11 to 90 percent a few days after the disaster. The President spoke to a Joint Session of Congress on Sept. 20 in clearly his finest moment. A President who had not even won the popular vote and who had often been accused of being the "accidental President"—a President who had frequently been thought not to be quite up to the job almost instantly became a giant in the White House.

Much of this would have been expected as America in peril has really nowhere to turn but the White House. But a great deal of the President's standing had to do with his own remarkable efforts. To virtually all informed observers, George W. Bush seemed to rise to the occasion—he seemed to indicate that sometimes in life a crisis can create a hero. America had found a President – a warrior-statesman. Interestingly a Gallup poll taken on Oct. 17 indicated that Americans would prefer, by a margin of 72 percent to 18 percent, George W. Bush to Bill Clinton as their Commander in Chief during the crisis. It is worth noting that President Clinton had left the White House in great controversy but with remarkably high approval ratings in virtually all polls.

The men and women closest to the President also rallied to the crisis. There was considerable public appreciation that the President had selected for his national security team such seasoned and experienced veterans not seeming to care if they would outshine or upstage him with the national press. General Powell, Dr. Rice, Secretary Rumsfeld, Vice-President Cheney, and former President Bush became the focal points of a supportive, thankful public. Also gone were the jokes about who was running the country—presidential advisers are important, vice-presidents are important—but in a real national crisis America is governed by its Commander in Chief and only its Commander in Chief. The entire world seemed to catch that lesson of American government immediately after Sept. 11, 2001.

One quiet, hidden figure was rarely in public view but almost certainly was central to all presidential activities. Dick Morris, a former Clinton aide, who very often seems to know what is happening inside the White House put it this way: throughout the crisis there was always "the last call"—the last call was President George W. Bush calling President George Herbert Walker Bush.

AMERICA LASHES BACK

On Oct. 7, 2001, 26 days after the attacks on New York and Washington, D.C. the United States lashed back at the terrorists with an intensive, elaborate military assault. B-1 bombers from Diego Garcia, B-2 bombers from Missouri, B-52 bombers from Germany and Diego Garcia, C-17s from Germany, as well as F-14s and F-18s from the carriers Enterprise and Carl Vinson struck Afghanistan in a broad, punishing strike. More than 150 planes were used the first day of what involved several days of air strikes. Approximately 50 cruise missiles were fired by British submarines and US ships in the Arabian Sea. Secretary Rumsfeld described the initial attacks as extremely successful. Obviously the American public agreed as the Gallup poll reported 90 percent approval of the President's action.

The targets of the American attack involved airfields, air defense systems, command and control systems, training camps, electrical/communications installations, military bases, and the ministry of defense. It is noteworthy that great care was taken not to hit areas that would involve large numbers of civilian casualties. The objectives of the attack were fairly clear—to destroy the Taliban, support the Northern Alliance as a possible replacement government, get the terrorists on the run, and clear the area for US/British Special Forces. Special Forces started their campaign on Oct. 19 when 100 Rangers assaulted the Taliban airfield in Kandahar. The Rangers went in at night, hit their targets, and returned to the safe confines of the USS Kitty Hawk within 12 hours.

The US military activities of October and November were largely successful. The operation went well—few US planes and personnel were lost. By Oct. 18 US and British Special Forces were roaming at will within Afghanistan. The northern cities had fallen to rebel forces and the Taliban defense of Kabul was nearing an end. Mazar-e-Sharif fell to the United Front on Nov. 11. The Taliban fled Kabul on Nov. 13. Ninety percent of Afghanistan was under anti-Taliban control by the end of November. By Dec. 22, all of Afganistan had been liberated. One hundred days of military strikes had eliminated the Taliban. The terrorists were totally routed with only remnants of their organization hiding in the caves of the south.

The US political objective was realized on Dec. 22. An interim government under the leadership of Hamid Karzai was established. The new government would serve for six months as the nation prepared for general elections. The political program would be followed by the massive economic reconstruction of Afghanistan. Public support continued. America's allies in the 40 nation Coalition remained remarkably loyal led by Great Britain's Prime Minister who seemed inspired by his role as the master diplomat maintaining Britain's new role in international politics as the primary bridge between Europe and the United States. All members of the Coalition and the UN recognized the new government of Afganistan.

The threats to success remained the same. The Coalition needed to constantly guard against their activities playing into the terrorists overall scheme which clearly was to have this campaign become a part of a broader war between the West and Islam. The fuel of the fire of a civilizational conflict would be the Arab-Israeli conflict. Osama bin Laden made quite clear in statements on Oct. 7 that he imagined the entire crisis to be a footnote to the Christian/Jewish plot to destroy Muslim culture in general and Islam in particular. The governments of Arabia quietly supported the Coalition but all watched the "Arab street" with extraordinary trepidation. Bin Laden, who had never shown much support for the Palestinian cause, was subtly changing the rules of the conflict—Muslim fundamentalism, which is largely unsupported in the world of Islam, would be replaced by the hatred of Israel as the new weapon in bin Laden's propaganda war.

What may have been Osama bin Laden's grand scheme began to emerge. He seemed to welcome the attack – apparently believing that somehow the Coalition would fail and that failure would spillover into the collapse of America's Arab Allies. In the end, Pakistan, Egypt, the Gulf States, and Saudi Arabia would be destroyed and captured by the terrorists. That end would bring about his grandest scheme—to acquire several states one of which, Pakistan, has a nuclear arsenal. From the caves of Afghanistan he would emerge as the head of a Pan-Islamist movement—a multinational state possessing the world's most frightening weapons. Bin Laden's fate was not clear by the winter of 2007. He may have perished in the caves of Afghanistan, but one thing was quite clear – his master plan had died at the hands of US military power.

America's ability to thwart the terrorist's grand scheme in the long run will be discussed later but in the end it will no doubt revolve around America's ability to endure. If the pro-Western Arab governments believe that America will remain committed to them and to the area, they will in all likelihood survive. If they believe that America and the Coalition which destroyed the Taliban, feel that justice has been done, and return to the safer confines of America and the West, then all may be lost. President Bush may have been thinking in such grand geo-strategic terms when he concluded his address to the nation on Oct. 7 with the statement that "we will not waiver, we will not falter, we will not tire, and we will not fail." Quite remarkably, the President added on Oct. 17 just as he boarded Air Force One for his trip to China that he knew at some point some Americans would tire of the War on Terrorism but that he never would—he would be there to the end—he would be there to lead the nation to victory.

WHAT CAUSED IT

The only absolute certainty about the cause of the attacks on New York and Washington, D.C. is that we do not know and will probably never know precisely why these horrendous events took place. Little doubt remained that the master terrorist behind the plot was Osama bin Laden, a former Saudi citizen and businessman, who has been the architect of many terrorist attacks over the last decade. Bin Laden lived or hid in Afghanistan and managed to create an international organization with cells, training centers, and campsites in roughly 60 countries. The general estimate was that his organization was worth billions of dollars and kept in its employ something in the range of 7000 "soldiers."

Perhaps the most difficult thing for the Western mind about the bin Laden attacks was that they were without demands. There was never any request or call for anything—just bloodshed and death. They took the nature of a war of all against all. The baffling question, therefore, is why—why would bin Laden have killed innocent civilians by the thousands and called for the death of millions without any direction to his activity?

One possible explanation may be a theory suggested in Dr. John Stoessinger's marvelous book, <u>Why Nations Go to War</u>. Dr. Stoessinger is a Professor of Political Science at the University of San Diego. He is a brilliant and wise man—he is a friend. John believes that there exists on this earth forms of evil which defy all explanation and all real understanding. He indicates that Hitler fell into that category. John has studied Hitler, from whom he and his mother escaped in the 1930s, for more than fifty years and has concluded that all civilized explanations fall short. Hitler was incomprehensibly evil—in Dr. Stoessinger's exact terms he was a "war lover"—a person who derived pleasure and satisfaction out of the death and misery of others.

Professor Stoessinger believes Saddam Hussein was another "war lover" who defied all understanding other than he was totally evil and enjoyed human suffering—especially the suffering which he brought about. Perhaps "war lover" is the explanation for Osama bin Laden—perhaps he wanted nothing more than the twisted satisfaction he derived from the terror he unleashed.

Another explanation may be related to the writings of Professor Samuel Huntington especially his thoughts in <u>The Clash of Civilizations</u>. Dr. Huntington believes that there are seven civilizations on this earth and that the wars and clashes of this century essentially will come along the fault lines of those civilizations. The primary hallmark of civilization is religion. He believes that the world's fastest growing civilization, Islam, has the greatest problems with the currently dominant West and therefore will present in varying ways the greatest problems for Western civilization in the future.

Islam it should be noted is not by its nature a religion of violence or terror. It is a religion like most others, which promotes peace, love, and human kindness. It is, however, a religion like many others which has within its giant umbrella many extreme elements—often called Muslim fundamentalists. The fundamentalists quite clearly regard the West as threatening to their values and their entire way of life. They quite clearly want the West and particularly its leader, the United States, out of the Middle East. Better yet they would like the West and America to be destroyed entirely because they are manifestations of evil, which defy the Koran, and the will of Allah. The talk of the restoration of the Caliphate could be quite ominous. The Caliphate, it should be remembered, in the 15th century included all of the Middle East, North Africa, and many parts of Europe. Israel is regarded as an appendage to the West and America and of course must also go. Perhaps Osama bin Laden was essentially a Muslim fundamentalist who was motivated primarily by that violent ideology.

It should be added that Islam has problems with the West regardless of the fundamentalists and much care and diplomacy will be required to manage these two magnificent civilizations through the troubled waters, which obviously lie ahead. Islam is uncomfortable with the Western doctrine of the separation of church and state and so far has produced not a single democracy in the Middle East with the possible exception of Iraq in 2006 and many would argue not a real democracy anywhere on earth. Individual freedom for men and women operationalized in the West through such doctrines as the separation of powers, division of powers, and judicial review are quite alien to Islam. With or without Osama bin Laden, America and its Allies may expect to have considerable trouble with Islam long into the future. All of these calculations are compounded by the extraordinary poverty of most Muslim nations. Saudi Arabia and the Gulf States are often the stereotype in the Western mind when in fact Jordan, Egypt, Syria and Palestine are the real pattern.

In the end we will never know why all of this happened to America. That will be frustrating and disappointing but should have little do to with America's response. It is essential to remember that most often in science we have solutions without fully or sometimes even partially understanding causes. Most medicine is based on finding cures to diseases such as polio, which have never been understood in terms of causes. In political policy it is worth noting that we did not understand Hitler but we knew what was needed—he had to be destroyed. We did not understand the "war lover" Stalin but we knew he had to be stopped. We did not understand Osama bin Laden but we knew how to cure the problem—in the words of Secretary Rumsfeld: "he had to be killed."

THE CALL TO ARMS

The most immediate reaction of the American government to the attacks of Sept. 11, 2001 was to protect the President, assess the nature of the attack, and to mobilize the chain of command for emergency conditions. The first few hours were unsettling on all counts. The reports from New York and the Pentagon suggested causalities vastly greater that the final result. Vice-President Cheney moved into the White House but the President was flown for hours from Florida to Nebraska to Indiana before it was believed safe enough for him to return to Washington. The White House and the Capitol were evacuated. Not surprisingly the secret service in particular and the government in general needed some time to collect themselves.

By the evening of Sept. 11 the President was securely in the White House and addressed the nation with a kind of calmness, determination, and fierceness that seemed to suit the moment perfectly. He announced the first night what was to become American policy for the long run—the terrorists would be apprehended, their organizations would be destroyed, all governments and international organizations would either cooperate in the War on Terrorism or they would be regarded as hostile to the United States. The homelands of terrorism would be the target.

In effect, the President declared war on terrorism. Perhaps even more interestingly and more unexpectedly he indicated what was to be the tone of his future agenda—the War on Terrorism would not involve a quick, flashy American response but rather would involve a national policy geared to rearranging all US foreign policy objectives for years to come. This war would be long, expensive, and bloody but in the end would be successful—he said, "we will not falter and we will not fail"-- America and the world quite clearly believed him.

The Americans immediately mounted a multi-faceted approach. Policies on every front were initiated from the criminal justice system to the armed forces, even to the creation of a new cabinet-level post for homeland security. More instructively, what seemed to emerge was a general battle plan that could alter America's overall position in the world for generations to come.

Behind the specific activities mentioned in the beginning of this essay, the President very quickly outlined a policy toward terrorism and the Middle East with several enduring qualities. In short, America very much as it had done in the 1940s, was going to be committed to a major military and economic presence in the Middle East permanently. In effect, the President seemed committed to the notion that the war against terrorism could not be allowed to collapse into a war between the West and Islam. America would need its Arab/Muslim friends to defeat terrorism—they in turn would need American military and economic support to maintain their regimes. In the end, Arabia and America had the same goal—it would be the final stand of the moderates against the extremists.

More specifically it seemed clear from the earliest stages that long-term military action against Afghanistan was inevitable. The Taliban and Osama bin Laden would be the targets. American policy would hope to catch and/or kill bin Laden but would be absolutely committed to toppling the Taliban. The Northern Alliance in northern Afghanistan would be the front line soldiers in the battle re-enforced by US and British Special Forces. Most importantly, a policy for the post-war reconstruction of Afghanistan would be started immediately. The US may be the only nation in the history of war that fought its way into a combat zone to drop food and medicine to the people whose government it was attacking.

In general terms the policy initiatives adopted at the initial parts of the campaign seemed to follow a certain pattern: phase one would focus on homeland security; phase two would pursue the criminal justice systems of America and Europe; phase three would call for military strikes against Afghanistan; phase four would refine and solidify an international coalition of nations and organizations to sustain the battle. What remained for the future were the next phases—some assumed, as hinted by Secretary Rumsfeld, that Saddam Hussein would be next on the list. Others hinted that Iraq, Iran, Syria, Libya, the Sudan, and other states, which had harbored and sponsored terrorism, might be military targets. Interestingly, the President notified the Security Council of the United Nations on Oct. 8, 2001 that the US might very well have to attack many states in order to defend itself. Perhaps even more revealing, the President identified what he called an "axis of evil" – Iran, Iraq, and North Korea in his State of the Union Address on Jan. 29, 2002.

What is clear as of this writing is that the extraordinary success of the first 100 days of military operations notwithstanding, America will be involved in the War on Terrorism for the indefinite future. The President is likely to focus on little else for the remainder of his presidency. The entire US government and American public opinion has been changed in the extreme. What seemed fascinating and important before Sept. 11, no longer captured the slightest attention.

ARMAGEDDON REVISITED

As difficult as the horror of Sept. 11, 2001 has been for America and its allies, a new even more frightening problem may be emerging. On Nov. 8, 2001 Osama bin Laden proclaimed to the world that his Al Qaeda organization possessed nuclear weapons and was quite prepared to use them. He had previously proclaimed that it is the religious duty of all Muslim states and organizations to acquire radiation weapons in order to balance similar weapons in the hands of the infidels. Secretary Rumsfeld commented the next day that he doubted bin Laden actually possessed nuclear weapons but did not question his desire to acquire and to use such devices. President Bush commented both during a press conference and before the UN General Assembly in November that weapons of mass destruction may in the end be the greatest threat facing the West.

If a nuclear device, approximately the size of a football, were used on an American target every human being within a radius of three to four miles would be killed. The number of deaths in an American city would be in the hundreds of thousands with thousands more injured by radiation. It is perhaps not a coincidence that since Sept. 11, Vice-President Cheney has been rarely within five miles of the location of the President. Three questions have to be addressed regarding the issue of nukes and terrorists—do the terrorists have the desire to acquire such weapons, if they had such weapons would they use them, and is it conceivable that they might be able to acquire such weapons? Tragically, the answer to all three questions is "yes."

Before Sept. 11, the nuclear age had undergone four phases. The first phase, 1945-1949, involved the American monopoly of nuclear devices following the attacks on Japan at the end of World War II. The second phase started in Oct. 1949 when the Soviets successfully exploded their first atomic device. A 20 year nuclear arms race between the US and the USSR followed. Phase three, 1949-1969, was represented by the SALT Treaties (Strategic Arms Limitation Treaties). During phase three the Soviets and Americans made substantial progress toward "freezing" their numbers of nuclear warheads. Nuclear weapons were not reduced in numbers but the nuclear arms race was ended. Phase four started with the introduction of START (Strategic Arms Reduction Treaties).

There have been three START treaties all moving the nuclear superpowers toward drastic reductions in their arsenals. At the beginning of the START process Russia and America had something in the range of

15,000 strategic warheads each reinforced by massive numbers of tactical warheads. By the end of START, it is anticipated that both of the nuclear superpowers will have cut their strategic warheads to something in the range of 2000 per nation representing cuts of nearly 80 percent. President Bush rather astoundingly announced at the Crawford, Texas summit on Nov. 14 that the US would reduce its strategic arsenal to between 1700 and 2200 warheads unilaterally within the next 10 years. President Putin responded, without mentioning a specific number, that the Russians would "match the US reductions."

Thus by Sept. 10, 2001 the world rather inappropriately seemed to believe that the nuclear genie had been put back in the bottle. Progress was reported on many fronts. Perhaps the most hopeful development involved the commitment by both Russia and America to totally eliminate all tactical nuclear warheads—"tacs" in some ways always represented the most frightening kind of ordinance in that the likelihood of their actually being used was always greater than the larger strategic warheads. America withdrew all tactical nuclear warheads from the fleet and overseas bases and the Russians were committed to a policy of destroying all of their tactical weapons with US financial assistance.

One serious problem lingered. By 2007 there were; two nuclear superpowers, Russia and America; three medium range nuclear powers, Great Britain, France, and China; and three "small" nuclear powers, India, Pakistan and Israel. More ominously there were at least four nations working on radiation programs—Algeria, Iran, North Korea and Syria. The latter represented the serious problem of nuclear proliferation. It should be noted with emphasis that all of the states pursuing nuclear programs have particularly hostile relations with America and the West. All of the four nations trying to develop "nukes" sponsor terrorism and are generally friendly to the most radical political elements in the Middle East.

Nevertheless, before Sept. 11 there was hope that through international agreements such as the non-proliferation treaty and cooperation among the five major nuclear powers the "genie" could still be contained. The Russians and the Americans had stabilized their rather frightening relationship at the nuclear level. The "balance of terror" could be managed by the continuation of MAD—Mutual Assured Destruction. MAD has always represented a form of nuclear deterrence; that is, a policy designed to stop something from happening.

The primary method of operationalizing MAD has been the presence of a Russian and American TRIAD. The TRIAD is a three-pronged nuclear system involving land, air, and sea missiles. By 2007, the Russians had about 6000 warheads on their ICBM (intercontinental ballistic missile), SLBM (submarine launched ballistic missile) and ALBM (air launched ballistic missile) fleets. The American number was approximately 8000. To repeat, both anticipated that in the not too distant future these numbers would be reduced to about 2000.

It should be noted that the Americans, originally inspired by President Reagan, have frequently expressed a willingness to eliminate all nuclear weapons if the rest of the world would do the same. This American idea is based more on the calculation that a nuclear-free world would enhance US strength rather than any movement toward nuclear pacifism. It must be added that a nuclear-free world is terribly unappealing to the Russians who regard their nuclear forces as the last element of bygone power. Moreover, the Russians curiously seem to believe that their nuclear forces represent a vital part of their national defense program. Russian nuclear forces account for almost 90 percent of Russian defense spending.

All of this is curious in the sense that the Russian Federation would seem to be more threatened by terrorism and insurrection, which can only be managed with the use of conventional forces. Moreover, the Russian nuclear forces, many of which have been in their silos for more than 20 years, are deteriorating dramatically. The numbers indicated above are totally deceiving. The West does not know how many Russian missiles could actually be delivered to their targets but the number is certainly not 6000—a few hundred is a more sensible calculation.

Sept. 11 may have changed most of the "rules of the nuclear game." From that point on it was very likely the world, in particular the established nuclear states, would regard "suitcase bombs" as more threatening than anything they might do to each other. The most likely defense against mega terrorism would seem rather obvious albeit terribly disturbing.

It is clearly impossible for the US to become a gigantic camp of search-dogs all trying to protect the nation from a bomb the size of a football. The only defense will no doubt be a determined offense. The terrorists and their weapons of mass destruction have to be destroyed—attack, not deterrence will have to be the battle cry of the future. The primary source of weapons-grade uranium is Russia. The disturbingly careless way the Federation manages such matters will no doubt become an immediate priority in America's new relationship with Russia. In the end, the presence of mega terrorism more than anything else may highlight the drastic changes brought to the world by the attacks on New York and Washington, D.C. Anthrax, bioterrorism, and car bombs will in all likelihood pale into insignificance compared to the prospect of millions of Western citizens dying in 21st century forms of nuclear Dresdens and Hiroshimas.

Another US national debate may be affected by the developments of 2001. President Bush has been committed to the development of an American ABM (antiballistic missile) defense system. He stated throughout the first parts of the War on Terrorism that his commitment continued. The Pentagon announced in March 2005 that several interceptor missiles would be deployed in Alaska and California during 2007 followed by efforts to expand the National Missile Defense System to the Navy and the Air Force. According to the President, the events of Sept. 11 illustrated that missile defense was more essential than ever in that America's enemies clearly will use such weapons if they have them. North Korea's firing of missiles capable of carrying nuclear weapons and its explosion of a nuclear weapon in 2007 drastically increased bipartisan support for the President's ABM system. Remarkably the US Senate, after decades of delay, passed a Resolution 98-0 encouraging the White House to proceed with "great dispatch" in the deployment of a US anti ballistic missile system.

PART II
TWO BALANCES OF POWER

American Middle East policy has always been easy to identify and almost impossible to operationalize. The United States wants from the Middle East, security for the state of Israel, and oil. Our Israeli policy was developed after World War II when we led the world toward the creation of the state of Israel in 1948. American motives then and now were primarily humanitarian resulting from the horrors of the holocaust and what in American eyes was the legitimate call on the part of the world's Jews for a part of their ancient homeland.

The US need for oil is a result of having a modern economy and most importantly our dependence on trade with sophisticated Allies such as Europe and Japan, which are almost entirely dependent on Gulf oil. America and its most important trading partners make up about 20 percent of the world's population but produce nearly 80 percent of its gross national product. Leaving aside the obvious moral questions related to a world of boundless prosperity and staggering poverty—a world where the rich are getting richer and the poor are either getting poorer or barely holding their own—there is absolutely no doubt that the energy resources of the Middle East are a vital part of Western prosperity. It is always important to recall that 60 percent of the known oil reserves of the planet are in the Middle East and that the bulk of that oil is in the Gulf. More to the point, all of the oil that the West will ever need is controlled by Saudi Arabia and the United Arab Emirates.

Both regimes are essentially vulnerable to the machinations of world terrorism. The Kingdom of Saudi Arabia with its dependence on approximately five million foreign workers is particularly disturbing to the West. The Saudi GNP, which was over $14,000 per capita in the mid 1990s, has dropped to about $7000 per person. Although the "permanent" stationing of 7000 US military personnel in the Kingdom ended in 2003, US-Saudi military cooperation is a constant source of trouble for the regime. Osama bin Laden forced the Saudis to do what is no longer acceptable to America—bribe the terrorists to do what they please as long as the Kingdom is untouched. It is important to note that perhaps one half of bin Laden's "troops" were Saudi by origin. They were in effect a foreign army occupying Afghanistan through their Taliban front.

BALANCE NUMBER 1

As a result, the United States has been in the business for 60 years of trying to maintain two, perhaps more accurately, two and a half balances of power in the region. The first balance is between Israel and the

Arab/Muslim world. The US is sensitive to shifts in the military balance that might put Israel in jeopardy. Israel has won all of its wars since 1948 including wars in 1948, 1956, 1967, 1973, and 1981, and they may be expected to do well in the current military conflict. Israel, however, only needs to lose one war and their survival will end. Egyptian President Nasser was correct: "we the Arabs" he argued, "Can lose 100 wars—we need only win the last one."

America's commitment to the first balance should not be confused with blind allegiance to Israel. The US has had and continues to have several quarrels with the Jewish state. The 1967 War has had the most enduring consequences for the Middle East. In that War the Israelis took all of the Sinai Peninsula, the Gaza Strip, all of the West Bank, the Golan Heights, and all of Jerusalem. The United Nations, and the United States to a lesser degree, has consistently supported the Arab position that Israel should return to its pre-1967 borders. Sinai was returned to Egypt as a result of the Camp David Accords in 1976. The West Bank and Gaza have been divided between Israel and the Palestinian Liberation Organization. There has been no progress on Golan with Syria and no progress regarding the city of Jerusalem. The differences between Israel and the US continue and may ultimately have a great deal to do with the outcome of America's War on Terrorism. President Bush has agreed in principle that there should be a Palestinian state.

The Israelis are divided on this issue but no doubt would like not to hear such broad suggestions by any American president. Bin Laden and other terrorists played constantly on the Arab suspicion of US/Israeli ties. America may be expected to plead, cajole, persuade and demand of Israel in this War, as it did during Desert Storm, to do everything possible to stay in the background and leave the battle to America and its Coalition partners. It is virtually impossible for America's traditional Arab allies to support a Coalition which includes the state of Israel.

During the spring of 2002, the delicate balance that the United States continually tries to maintain between Israel and its Arab neighbors gave all the appearances of totally collapsing. The Intifadah or "Uprising," which started 18 months earlier, had claimed about 400 Israeli and 1600 Palestinian lives. On April 15, 2002 President Bush's special envoy to the area, Marine Corps General Zinni, seemed on the brink of arranging a ceasefire between Israel and the Palestinian Authority. It was generally assumed the ceasefire would ultimately lead to the realization of the Tenet and Mitchell Plans for peace. The Tenet Plan was named after CIA Director George Tenet and outlined a series of confidence building measures such as intelligence sharing, military withdrawal schedules, and predetermined multilateral conferences that would stop the fighting and lead to the Mitchell Plan. The Mitchell Plan was named after former Senate Majority leader George Mitchell and essentially outlined an arrangement that called for the coexistence of Israel with an independent, sovereign Palestine under Palestinian control. The Mitchell Plan called for a divided Jerusalem, open trade, unrestricted access to major religious sites and implied an end to Israeli settlements in the West Bank.

The entire process was given an added, historic boost during the 22 nation Arab summit of April during which Crown Prince Abdullah of Saudi Arabia proposed full recognition of Israel by all Arab nations in exchange for the independence of Palestine. The Tenet, Mitchell, and Saudi plans all lacked precise details but did offer a framework for future peace. It seemed particularly hopeful and important that the Arab summit for the first time since the creation of Israel called upon all Islam to recognize the permanent right of the Jewish state to exist.

Just as the peace process seemed to take on new life, a Palestinian suicide bomber killed 28 Israelis celebrating Passover in a hotel in Netanya. Roughly another 150 Israelis were seriously injured. The Passover Massacre was followed by 7 days of suicide bombings claiming scores of Israeli lives. The ceasefire peace proposals died as the Israelis retaliated with more force than they had used since the 1973 war. Hundreds of Israeli tanks and roughly 16,000 soldiers of the IDF (the Israeli Defense Force) moved into the West Bank and Gaza ultimately reoccupying the entire region. Prime Minister Sharon announced that Israel was at War, its very survival was at stake, and that the enemy was the Palestinian Authority led by Arafat whom he once again labeled a terrorist. The Israelis rolled over the Palestinians finally isolating Arafat within three rooms of his headquarters in Ramallah. The "Arab street" erupted with massive anti American and anti Israeli demonstrations exploding in nearly every Arab capitol. Particularly disturbing to the United States was the fact that Arab reaction included America's traditional allies such as Jordan, Egypt, Saudi Arabia and the Gulf States. Bahrain, the home of the American fleet in the Persian Gulf and a long standing American ally, was unusually explosive causing all American personnel to be confined to their ships and bases.

The United Nation's Security Council passed a resolution 14-0 with US support calling for the Israelis to withdraw from the occupied lands. President Bush guardedly supported Israel but essentially stood alone as the European Union, the Vatican and most nations around the world condemned the Israeli reaction as excessive, brutal, and illegal. Israel's critics almost universally called upon Israel to return to its pre-1967 borders meaning to withdraw permanently from the West Bank, the Golan Heights, Gaza, and East Jerusalem.

On April 4, the President dispatched Secretary of State Powell to the region indicating the American administration feared the situation was spiraling out of control. Powell's mission was of course to try to stop the fighting which the President knew would be nearly impossible. Also of considerable importance was the goal of containing the crisis so that it did not spill over into the entire region. Secretary Powell met with Prime Minister Sharon and Chairman Arafat as well as several Arab/Muslim leaders. The end result was the beginning of a new dialogue with some prospect of a cease-fire. The US no doubt did not expect this arrangement to be much more successful than the 12 cease-fires which preceded it but did have reason to hope that the Israeli-Palestinian crisis could be confined to that area alone thereby not disrupting overall American goals regarding the Middle East and the War on Terrorism. The primary goal of US diplomacy was to thwart the Iranian, Iraqi, and Syrian plans to once again use the Palestinians, for whom they have traditionally had very little sympathy, as a diversion to keep the US and its Coalition away from them.

The entire matter was compounded by new information that Arafat had been in the business of secretly supporting the suicide attacks while negotiating with the US and Israel about peace. Perhaps even more ominous, it became clear in April that Iraq, Iran, and Syria had been encouraging and financially supporting the suicide attacks. Saddam Hussein proudly announced on April 2 his intention to raise the dollars Iraq would give to the families of suicide bombers to an extraordinary $25,000. The Iraqi dictator also announced the next day that Iraq would end all oil shipments to the West for one month or until the Israelis withdrew from Palestine. He called on other Muslim states, none of which responded, to use oil to force America's hand. Interestingly, National Security Adviser Condi Rice responded by stating she hoped the "Iraqis would enjoy eating oil."

With the announcement of Secretary Powell's involvement, President Bush called on Israel to immediately withdraw from the West Bank and Gaza. The President repeated his contention that Arafat had not done enough to stop the terrorists. The President most dramatically was trying to restore the status quo ante—he proclaimed that "enough is enough" and the violence had to stop. He was doing what American Presidents have been doing for 60 years—he was trying to maintain at least the appearance of fairness so that in the end the US could broker a peace settlement to the crisis. The President was particularly stern in his warning to "outsiders" such as Iran, Iraq, and Syria to stay out of the situation. He repeated his warning that those who sponsor terrorism are terrorists themselves and will ultimately face US retribution.

Very little seemed clear by early 2004 as to the final outcome of the bloodletting. The positions of the major actors however were becoming clear and will probably hold the keys to the future. Prime Minister Sharon and former Prime Minister Netanyahu seemed fixed on the idea that Arafat would never be an appropriate partner in peace. Netanyahu in the name of the Israeli government called for his removal from office and forced exile. He referred to Arafat as a "murdering butcher" who was personally responsible for the killing of scores of Israeli civilians. In effect, Arafat they argued was part of the problem and would never be part of the solution. He always was and would always be a terrorist bent on the destruction of the Jewish state. All gestures of peace toward the PLO would be interpreted as "signs of weakness" and would only encourage terrorism. Former Prime Minister Barak joined in by noting that Israel had offered Arafat enormous concessions at Camp David in 1999 and received the "Uprising" in response.

According to this argument, Israel must attack the terrorists very much as the US went after Al Qaeda. Someday off in the distant future the punishment of the terrorists and the destruction of their infrastructure might bring about a new Arab/Palestinian approach. The Prime Minister seemed to believe that Israel had no choice—war today and negotiations in a far away tomorrow. This "hardline" position, it should be noted, seemed to gain ascendancy with the Israeli public with each new suicide bomber. Sharon, who was never a charismatic leader, reached nearly 80 percent approval rating in Israeli public opinion polls after the invasion.

The full depth of the problem was indicated by the corresponding level of support for Arafat among the Palestinians. Arafat only weeks before was generally thought "to be on his way out" and regarded as irrelevant to regional politics. At the end of April, revealingly, Saddam Hussein renamed one of the largest boulevard's in Baghdad for Yasser Arafat and proclaimed him to be the "Lion of Arabia." Arafat became a "national" hero to the Palestinian refugees who have long represented the most desperate part of the problem. There are 3.9 million Palestinian refugees in the area, of which 2.1 million live in the appalling camps located in Lebanon, Jordan, Syria and the West Bank. Although the United Nations spends $414 million per year most of which is donated by the US and

Europe, the refugees have never had anything but the most contemptuous view of America and Israel. The camps are always the lightening rod of every Israeli-Palestinian crisis. Interestingly, the Arab world provides practically no assistance to the camps and has been quite satisfied for more than 50 years to keep the Palestinians trapped in these Middle Eastern "Bantustans." Horrifyingly, both sides of the battle seemed locked into conflict supported overwhelmingly by their respective publics.

The alternative view, represented by the Bush Administration, remained committed to the peace process. Although Arafat had lost most of his credibility with the US and the President called for his "removal" from power, the PLO was still regarded as "the only game in town." Moreover, in keeping with the "law of unexpected consequences" the total destruction of the PLO might be even more destabilizing. More importantly, the President indicated that he believed that Sharon's reoccupation of the West Bank was not in Israelis long-term security interests meaning there was no reasonable end-game to the policy. Unlike the American campaign in Afghanistan, Israel represented an occupying army trying to subdue three million Palestinians most of whom hated both Israel and the occupation. Going after the Palestinian terrorist infrastructure in the form of Hizballah, Hamas, and the Islamic Jihad, no matter how legitimate from Israel's perspective, would inevitably be interpreted in Palestine and throughout the region as an imperial war against the people of Palestine.

In the end the Americans believed, Israel was both threatening its own security and becoming a strategic liability to the US. Instead of helping America in its War on Terrorism, Israel was solidifying the ranks of the terrorists indeed perhaps even increasing their numbers and increasing the likelihood that the US itself would become the target of a whole new range of terrorist organizations. America's enemies would increase not decrease and would include not just fundamentalist organizations such as Al Qaeda but all terrorist organizations committed to the cause of the Palestinians.

Finally, the Sharon, Netanyahu, Likud scheme threatened to destabilize the entire region. Instead of destroying the terrorists, Israel might manage to destroy America's Allies in the region. The most vulnerable were obviously Jordan, Saudi Arabia, Egypt, and the Gulf States. Israeli leadership in 2002 seemed to be committed to a war of "all against all" with Israel staking its very survival on its own resources plus US support. Netanyahu proclaimed during his spring visit to the US that Israel would "clean up" Palestine and America should take care of Saddam. He added that in the end all Arab regimes were suspect, all in one form or another had supported terrorists, and all should be replaced by democratic governments.

President Bush clearly did not regard this as an acceptable gamble and/or strategy. In a certain sense the Israelis and the Americans were disputing tactics rather than strategy. Both were committed to the destruction of terrorism, both regarded Arafat as quite prepared to use terrorist methods, both believed the PLO had to be reformed, and both regarded Iraq, Iran, and Syria as the primary culprits in this nightmarish "dance of death." The difference between Israel and the US revolved around how to proceed tactically—Israel was prepared to confront a regional conflagration and the Americans were not. The President still believed that America's traditional Arab/Muslim allies were essential to final victory. America's policy toward Israel, not very subtly, was committed to the idea that Israel "must get out of the way" for the larger battles to come.

In the end, only one solution seemed possible. Israel and Palestine are joined by destiny and geography and must cooperate or face endless conflict and bloodshed. There really was no solution other than coexistence represented by two states living next to each other sharing the same resources and the same religious symbols. There were four parts to the extraordinarily complicated conflict: the status of Jerusalem, the status of the Palestinian refugees, the status of the Israeli settlements, and the status of an independent Palestine. But in the end, Israel did not want and could not destroy and/or occupy all of Palestine. The Palestinians could not and would not be allowed to "run the Jews back into the sea." Ironically and quite tragically the solution to the Israeli-Palestinian crisis was obvious and unavoidable—two states, Israel and Palestine, would have to live side by side. What was not clear was how long the nightmarish process would take.

The Uprising of 2002 also presented America and its allies with one other enormously complicated set of options. The general wisdom of the day argued that Iraq, Iran, and Syria although clearly sponsoring terrorism and clearly threatening to the West, could only be dealt with once some kind of resolution of the crisis in Palestine had been realized. America, most observers argued, could not become engaged in war throughout the region and obviously faced the problem of stretching its forces too thinly from Afghanistan to Palestine. No matter how threatening Iraq in particular might be, America's desire to deal with that problem would have to wait for another day.

The counter view, which was clearly the view of the President of the United States, was that Saddam's regime was dangerous to America, it was growing more dangerous each day, and ironically Iraq was at the root of the problems in Palestine. As long as the US and Israel were chasing Hamas and Hizballah without confronting the source of the problem they were confusing tactics with strategy. Iraq would have to be dealt with in the very immediate future. It was noteworthy that by the summer of 2002 US forces deployed in the Middle East and South Asia reached nearly 100,000 as compared to the usual 20,000.

It seemed clearer each day that the American President had his sights on Iraq regardless of the machinations of the crisis in Palestine. Indeed, he seemed to believe that the road to peace in Palestine ran through Baghdad and not the West Bank. The President's view prevailed with the destruction of the Iraqi regime in 2003. America turned its attention back to the Palestinian question. Syria and Iran were put on "notice" that further disruption of the peace process would not be tolerated. The US announced its "roadmap" for peace after the fall of Baghdad. The roadmap called for concessions on both sides – the goal was clear – there would be an American sponsored Palestine but it would be democratic and dedicated to peace. Israel would be secure but it would have to revise drastically its policies toward Israeli settlements. Chairman Arafaat's death in November 2004, which was followed by the election of moderate PLO leaders, increased dramatically the chances of success for the American peace plan. Interestingly, Prime Minister Sharon committed Israel to full withdrawal from Gaza. Astoundingly, events in the Middle East took an even more unexpected turn when the citizens of Lebanon demanded and achieved Syrian withdrawal from their country. Finally, by early 2006 the Israeli government seemed committed to the American position regarding an independent Palestine. The almost bizarre nature of the Israeli-Palestinian question took a more negative turn with the election of a Hamas government In Palestine in 2006. Shortly thereafter Prime Minister Sharon was incapacitated with a massive stroke. The new Israeli government continued to build a wall separating Israel and the West Bank. The summer of 2006 indicated the totally explosive nature of the problem. Israel and Hizballah engaged in a full military confrontation which settled nothing. Peace with the Palestinians and protection from the terrorists would be Israel's immediate goals – final resolution of the conflict would have to wait for another day.

It should be noted that America's role as the balancer between Israel and the Arabs was most dramatically demonstrated by the Yom Kippur War of 1973-74. The Arabs caught Israel by surprise, stormed across Suez and were generally succeeding at the outset of the battle. American policy at that point was pro-Israeli. As the Israelis turned the tide and ran the Egyptians, in particular the Egyptian 3rd army into Sinai threatening its elimination, the US became pro-Egyptian.

The remarkable skills of Henry Kissinger and Richard Nixon carried the day. The era of shuttle diplomacy allowed both sides a way to withdraw from the precipice. It is vital to note that Israel today has better relations with Egypt than any other Arab nation. It is important to note that not coincidentally Egypt and Israel receive more US aid than any other two nations on earth. America in 1973 demonstrated its skills as a "balancer." In the spirit of Disraeli, the balancer never asks who is right or wrong—the balancer always asks who is strong and who is weak. In order to maintain the balance, the balancer will always support the weak. President Bush's policies of 2004-2006 were designed to accomplish the same goal—to bring peace to the Middle East because it is in America's strategic interest to have peace in the region and because peace between Israel and Palestine would allow the US to more effectively pursue its global objectives in the War on Terror.

BALANCE NUMBER 2

The second balance involves the American attempt to align itself with the conservative or moderate Arab states such as Saudi Arabia, Jordan, Egypt and the Emirates in their struggle with the radical Arab/Muslim states such as Syria, Iran, and until 2003, Iraq. The conservatives have long been engaged in a deadly struggle with the radicals.

Iraq and Iran imagine themselves as the "natural" leaders of the region. Although Iran is not Arab, the leadership since 1979 seems totally committed to spreading Muslim fundamentalism throughout the region, which of course it will try to control. While Saddam was in power, Iraq moved toward a day when it could replace Iran as the hegemon of the area. Iran's response to the War on Terrorism may provide a fascinating clue to the future. Once the US bombing of Afghanistan began the Iranians announced that the entire military operation was "totally unacceptable." A few days later, the new fairly moderate President of Iran, indicated that Americans forced to land in Iran would be provided with safe haven and returned to their comrades.

Iraq's response did not involve such subtleties. Saddam sided with the Taliban immediately and steadfastly. Although Iran has harbored and sponsored terrorists in the past they have traditionally hated the Taliban. Iran is massively complicated, in effect having three governments none of which seems to be in charge. Iran nevertheless will be one of the keys to America's future in the area. President Bush probably had Iran in mind when he implied at the end of October 2003 that all nations would be given a "pass," a second chance on terrorism regardless of past behavior if they helped the US now. Even Iraq might be tempted to change course. It could not have been pleasant for terror-sponsoring states to watch the Taliban liquated each night on the evening news. The general direction of America's policy toward the radicals was complicated but clear: America would threaten the "axis of evil" and be prepared for military conflict but would allow for improved relations for as long as possible. The radicals would not be allowed to continue to develop weapons of mass destruction and would not be allowed to indulge in state-sponsored terrorism. They would be, however, allowed to change. When it became clear in 2003 that Iraq would not change, Operation Iraqi Freedom was started. After Saddam's regime was destroyed, Iran was put on notice that the US would not allow Tehran to develop weapons of mass destruction. Also, the US not very subtly indicated its support for democratic revolution within Iran. Importantly, the Iranian government agreed to the EU – 3 plan for restricting Iranian nuclear programs to peaceful purposes at the end of 2004. Iranian policy became even more bizarre in 2005-2006 when the new fundamentalist President announced "Israel should be wiped off the face of the earth" and recommitted the nation to the development of nuclear energy. President Bush responded by asserting that America believed a diplomatic solution was possible regarding Iran but the use of military force "was still on the table." The US and the EU turned to the UN in 2006 and 2007 which called for a boycott of Iran until it stopped its enrichment program.

American policy has been committed, through the exercise of extraordinary military power, to maintain the conservative regimes of Saudi Arabia, Bahrain, Kuwait, the U.A.E., Qatar, and Oman. The conservative states have the oil but they also have terrible problems. All are dictatorships, all wrestle with Shiite extremists within their borders, all are militarily weak, all are dependent on foreign labor, which has utterly no loyalty to any of them, and all have made "deals" with terrorists. All live in great peril and all are terrified of the fundamentalists. All are caught along with the United States in the middle of a nightmarish dilemma—without the United States they will in all likelihood be crushed—with America they may appear to have sold their souls to the infidels and doom themselves whatever else they do.

The half balance involved the United States' attempt to play Iraq, Syria, and Iran off against each. It might be thought of from the American perspective as the "balance of the bastards." The United States disliked them all, they of course reciprocated, and we tried to keep all of them afloat so that no one dominated. "The evil we know may be better than the evil we can imagine" may be the best description of this part of the traditional American policy. The half balance changed dramatically in 2003 with the elimination of Saddam Hussein. The radicals were left with only Syria and Iran, both of which were surrounded by US forces.

As bizarre as it may seem, American policy in the Middle East has worked reasonably well. Israel flourishes and its survival seems secure. The oil is flowing and the conservative states for the moment are quite stable. The primary threat for the future is Muslim fundamentalism particularly in the perverted form of terrorism. It is quite difficult for Westerners to understand the Muslim commitment to religion, even the more moderate forms of Islam. It appears to be a strange combination of religion, politics, and culture. It is unbelievably intense and it is completely pervasive. For Westerners it is a little frightening. Women have few political rights—whole societies have few rights which Westerners take for granted. In the name of Islam, politics is placed in a position of almost absolute tyranny. We are, with considerable justification, both religiously and politically, very threatening to Islam. If they reform or Westernize, the world as they know it will disappear—if they do not, they may very well destroy each other.

The second great threat to the region is American public opinion. Prior to Sept. 11 both American political parties had substantial minorities, which would like "to bring the boys home." The left sees American problems as compelling and foreign policy is not on their list. The right sees our current level of world involvement as dangerous and expensive. The left wants to save "spotted owls" and the right wants to "get the government off the backs of the American people." Before Sept. 11 both were headed in the same direction regarding the Middle East. Both wanted America to withdraw and let the Arabs, the Japanese, and the Europeans fend for themselves. Both were wrong. Of course Sept. 11 has muted the isolationists in both parties but isolationism is an American tradition, which will be hard to dismiss. Although both presidential candidates in 2004 were committed on the War on Terror and the War in Iraq, both the Republicans and the Democrats had to often wrestle with the isolationists in their ranks. By 2006, calls for withdrawal from Iraq increased in both parties. Public support for the war in Iraq declined dramatically. Interestingly, none of the major presidential candidates for 2008 called for an abrupt American end to the war. The midterm election of 2006 increased calls for a change in US policy toward Iraq. The Baker Commission brought forth proposals the President agreed to consider.

It is quite possible that Americans will grow weary of the War on Terrorism and demand a return to normalcy. It is always worth recalling that the US is an island geopolitically surrounded by two safe oceans and two friendly, weak neighbors. We think like an island people. Our island mentality is reinforced by the fact that Americans speak the world's language and use the world's currency and therefore see little reason to become involved in international politics. It is always important to remember that America remained neutral during the 1930s while Japan and Germany conquered much of Asia and Europe. Had the Japanese not made the colossal mistake of attacking Pearl Harbor, the Fascists might very well have won the War. If Osama bin Laden had not made the colossal mistake of attacking New York and Washington, D.C., America might have remained on the sidelines of world terrorism until it was too late. The open question with America will always be how long can the nation sustain its interest in expensive, frightening foreign engagements.

If the United States should withdraw from the Gulf, the entire region would descend into a kind of Dark Age from which it might never recover. Western economic activity would be terribly disrupted. America for good or for ill is the natural peacemaker of the Middle East and all the key players know it. America's desire to maintain 2 ½ balances is best served by the absence of military conflict. America is the peacemaker not because it represents the "good guys" but because peace is in America's interest. For as long as one can see into the future, it will be in our interest to maintain our influence in the region in effect turning the Arabian Gulf into a kind of "American lake" from which the entire world will benefit. As Senator Hillary Clinton noted in 2006 and President Bush repeated on scores of occasions, it would be completely disastrous to come home regardless of how tempting that might be. Most of the key political players in the US agreed in 2007 that an American defeat in Iraq would lead to a kind of Taliban government in Iraq and that terrorists throughout the world would be "inspired" to more and more violence. The American debate for the moment was about tactics not strategy. The War on Terrorism will not last forever— ironically permanent victory in that war may require that America's commitment to the Middle East must last forever.

The conservative/moderate regimes have a reasonable chance of surviving and even of destroying the terrorists in their midst with Western help—they have none without it.

PART III
OPERATION IRAQI FREEDOM

THE WINDS OF WAR

By the fall of 2002, it became clear that the American Administration had given up any hope of successfully following a policy of containing the Iraqi regime of Saddam Hussein. President Bush spoke to the nation on the anniversary of the Sept. 11 attack and again the next day to the General Assembly of the United Nations. He noted with pride that the US had not been hit by terrorists in more than a year, that the Taliban had been evicted from Afghanistan, that approximately one-third of the Al Qaeda leadership had been detained or arrested, that America had established cooperative relationships with more than 100 nations which had detained more than 3000 possible terrorists, that hundreds of millions of dollars of Al Qaeda funds had been blocked, and that large amounts of information had been confiscated from secret Al Qaeda sources. Both speeches, however, focused less on the accomplishments of the past than the idea that the US was moving slowly, deliberately, carefully but without question toward war.

Saddam Hussein was regarded as a serious threat to regional security in the Middle East as well as a future threat to America and its Allies. The President noted ominously that Saddam had warred upon his neighbors and his own people for more than 25 years and had consistently thwarted the will of the international community by continuing to develop weapons of mass destruction. He outlined 10 years of Iraqi violations of more than 16 mandatory resolutions of the Security Council of the United Nations. He reviewed Iraq's "decade of defiance" includes its total contravention of UN Resolutions 686, 687, 688, and 1373. He noted with some special emphasis that Saddam's regime had not only invaded two of its neighbors, Iran in 1980, and Kuwait in 1990; used chemical weapons against Iran and the Kurds; tortured large numbers of its own citizens; ordered the extermination of all males between the ages of 12 and 70 in northern Iraq; but in 1993 had tried to assassinate the Emir of Kuwait and a former President of the United States. The former President, the world knew, was President George W. Bush's father—President George Herbert Walker Bush. The President made it abundantly clear to the UN that if the world organization would not move immediately and effectively to deal with a regime that was putting at risk millions of innocent lives, the United States would be quite prepared to act unilaterally.

Moreover, Iraq by the fall of 2002 was thought to be one of the primary examples of a regime harboring, training, and financing terrorist's organizations--a direct contravention of the Bush Doctrine outlined shortly after the attacks on New York and Washington, D.C. The President repeated his statement of Sept. 20, 2001: "Either you are with us or you are with the terrorists. From this day forward, any nation that continues to harbor or support terrorism will be regarded . . . as a hostile regime."

On Sept. 12, 2002 President Bush made several demands before the UN concerning Iraq: 1) Iraq must immediately eliminate all weapons of mass destruction; 2) Iraq must totally end the suppression of its own people; 3) Iraq must return all prisoners from the Gulf War; 4) Iraq must totally compensate the nations it has warred upon; 5) and Iraq must end its subversion of the "oil for food" program. Put most directly, Saddam's Iraq was a threat because of four considerations: the history of the regime; the history of Saddam's leadership; Iraq's robust pursuit of chemical, bacterial, and nuclear weapons; and the regimes quartering and sponsoring of terrorists organizations. It must be emphasized that the President in his remarkably hawkish presentation to the UN, was not calling for a return of UN inspectors to Baghdad, rather he was calling for the immediate elimination of the regime of Saddam Hussein. Almost gratuitously the President added that once his demands were met, the US and the UN would be delighted to supervise elections in Iraq.

The Iraqi response to the President's UN speech was predictable and clever. They condemned America once again for its imperialist designs on Iraqi oil, its constant interference in the affairs of a sovereign nation, and its overall threat to the world of Islam. Baghdad added, however, that UN inspectors would be allowed to return to Iraq without any restrictions or preconditions. In a familiar fashion, Saddam's spokesman defined "unconditional" to mean there would in fact be several conditions. The UN inspectors would not be allowed to inspect Saddam's eight presidential palaces without prior notice and without Iraqi permission. It should be noted that the presidential palaces are not what the term implies. The eight so-called palaces involved more than twenty square miles with roughly 1000 buildings. Moreover, the UN inspectors would be "unconditionally" restricted by all the problems and bureaucratic ploys that had rendered their work before 1998 to be almost entirely worthless.

The President indicated to the nation that he intended to seek Congressional approval of his actions in the form of a Congressional Resolution. On Sept. 20, 2002 the President submitted to Congress a Joint Resolution that allowed the President to use whatever methods he deemed appropriate, including military force, to bring total Iraqi compliance with all UN and US resolutions. It is important to note that the Congress in 1998 under the sponsorship of the Clinton Administration had overwhelmingly supported a resolution calling for the "liberation of Iraq." In effect, President Bush was not calling for an entirely new American approach to Baghdad rather he was calling for procedures that would realize the objectives of policies agreed to at the end of Desert Storm and consistently supported by the UN and the Congress from 1991 to 2002.

The November elections were not thought to be an appropriate reason to delay Congressional consultation. The President clearly was prepared to accept the criticism of some that he was forcing the opposition into a difficult or impossible situation. Instead the President was prepared to rest his case on precisely the opposite calculation--nothing could be more appropriate than discussing the most serious issue facing the nation before the elections were held. In effect, the November Congressional elections became something of a national plebiscite on America's War policy.

The Congressional Democratic Party was in the most difficult position. Most Democrats did not want to be "caught" on the side of questioning the Commander in Chief with war so close but the leadership had to try to reconcile the large number of Congressional Democrats who were opposed to any military action. The Republicans rather obviously had no such problem as they were prepared to support almost any wartime resolution requested by the President. During the second week of October, 2002, the matter was resolved. Both houses of Congress passed overwhelmingly a Resolution of War (the Senate 77-23 and the House 296-108) which called upon the President to move in whatever way he decided toward removing Iraq as a threat to regional security, America's Allies, and the US itself. For America at least, the Winds of War were at hand.

The President in the fall also determined that it would be appropriate to return one more time to the United Nations for support and consultation. Interestingly the President and Prime Minister Blair made it abundantly clear that they believed the UN had already spoken to this question several times in the past, most recently with the UN resolutions of 1998 which had called for UN inspectors to be allowed into Iraq at "any time without any qualifications." The President and the Prime Minister went further with their joint communiqué after the Camp David summit of Sept. 5 which stated that if UN support were not forthcoming the US and the United Kingdom were quite prepared to act alone. The President restated his general view on Oct. 4 that the "United Nations must either stand with us or stand aside." He repeated his overall assessment supported by the Prime Minister that the UN was facing a critical, perhaps fateful moment in its history. If the UN could not help resolve the problem poised by Saddam Hussein then it might not be able to carry on with its historic mission of maintaining the peace and order of the world. If it were not able to respond to this crisis, it would no doubt follow the path of the League of Nations which collapsed in the 1930s in the face of fascist aggression.

The Americans and the British also challenged the moral authority of the UN albeit knowing that UN approval would be popular both within the US and the UK. Both President Bush and Prime Minister Blair explained their view that UN support meant support within the UN Security Council which meant the support of the five permanent members—the US, France, Russia, China, and Great Britain. Contrary to public perception throughout much of the world, the UN in a crisis involves only the votes of its five permanent members. The General Assembly of 190 nations is almost entirely irrelevant falling into its traditional role as the "talk shop" of the world. In effect, the so-called moral authority of the UN regarding the Iraqi crisis involved the possible vetoes of only France and Russia, which were far more concerned with retrieving past debts from the Iraqis totaling more than $20 billion, than any vague references to international law.

UN involvement in October 2002 was confused even more by the UN agreement with Iraq to send inspectors into the area under the old, unworkable resolutions. On Oct. 14, Secretary Powell announced from the UN that he had "managed" to persuade the UN to drop this approach. By November the US had persuaded the Security Council to pass a new resolution calling for full Iraqi disarmament reinforced by the threat of military action. The Security Council voted unanimously (15-0) on Nov. 8, 2002 for Resolution 1441 stating that Iraq was in violation of numerous, binding UN resolutions; that Iraq would be allowed one last chance to disarm by eliminating all of its weapons of mass destruction; a new inspection regime would be established with the authority to "go anywhere at anytime;" and further Iraqi violations would bring about "serious consequences." French and American quarrels about a two tiered approach to the problem were set aside. The Security Council expected that America and Great Britain would consult with New York before taking military action but nothing in the resolution required formal UN approval. Few expected Saddam's government to comply—the Winds of War had reached New York.

It is important to note the impact the US Congressional elections of Nov. 5 had on the Security Council three days before it voted on its "final" resolution concerning Iraq. The midterm election of 2002 should properly be placed in the category of the utterly astounding. Presidents lose on the average 30 seats in the House and 8 seats in the Senate during the first election after they assume office. No Republican President in the history of the United States has ever gained Congressional seats during his first midterm election—only one has managed this task since the Civil War—Franklin Delano Roosevelt.

On Nov. 5, 2002 Americans went to the polls in what most observers "knew" would be a "normal" election with the President's Party possibly holding the House but most definitely losing ground in the Senate. When the excitement calmed—the Republicans had routed the Democrats in both Chambers of Congress. Ten Senate seats of the 34 up for election were considered "too close to call." The Republicans won eight losing South Dakota by only 522 votes and the tenth, Arkansas, involved almost entirely the personal affairs of the Republican Senator. Thus the Republicans had control of the US Senate by a margin of 51 to 48 (one independent). Moreover, the Republicans gained five seats in the House increasing their majority from 223 to 228 leaving the Democrats with 206 (one independent).

Senator Daschle was removed as majority of the Senate turning that position over to Senator Lott of Mississippi and Congressman Gephardt suffered his fourth straight defeat in an attempt to become Speaker of the House. Minority Leader Gephardt resigned from the Democratic leadership the next day and was shortly thereafter replaced by Nancy Pelosi of California. It is essential to recall that the majority party in Congress appoints all the chairmen of all the committees and subcommittees. For the first time in more 50 years, the Republicans controlled the White House, the US House of Representatives, and the US Senate.

President Bush ignored the advice of many of his most senior advisers and waged into the battle. In effect he was risking his enormous popularity and prestige by personally directing the campaign. In the three weeks preceding the election, the President barnstormed the nation for his candidates. He visited 17 states several times, personally selected several of the key candidates, and raised more than $140 million for the Republican "war chest." Obviously his gamble paid off. President Bush finished his first term with an extremely cooperative Republican majority and a stunned Democratic minority. The President's plans for education, massive judicial appointments, a department of homeland security, continued tax cuts, and foreign policy initiatives of the boldest kind were secure.

US elections are impossible to predict and almost as difficult to sort out once they have been completed. The general view about November 2002 is that the American public did what it always does—voted its "pocket book." Democratic losses therefore were a result of the Democrats not providing the nation with a viable economic alternative to the Republicans regarding the many economic difficulties facing the nation. There is, no doubt, some truth in this view, but the election was really more about two entirely different calculations: US foreign policy and George W. Bush. Regarding the President, George W. Bush in November 2002 had the highest, longest running approval ratings in the history of the Presidency that probably can be explained fairly simply. The American people liked him—genuinely liked him. The general view seemed to be that he was legitimate, straightforward, bright, comfortable with himself, moderate, and most of all exuded a kind of straightforward approach to life missing in the modern Presidency. Secretary of State Shultz once said: "honesty is the coin of the realm." Most Americans seemed to believe that their President was an honest, terribly nice, terribly decent man—"what you see is what you get" and in his case that was apparently quite a lot.

Perhaps even more importantly, the American people seemed to sense that they were headed for difficult times particularly in terms of international affairs. They seemed quite ready to trust the President to guide the nation effectively through this moment of destiny—angry people turn against their government—anxious people do not. The American people on Nov. 5, 2002 seemed ready to put their hopes for the nation, their families, and their lives in the hands of the President of the United States. George W. Bush had his mandate—the mandate that had so painfully eluded him in election of 2000. All of this was being observed with extraordinary interest around the world and particularly in the halls of the UN. America's critics and no doubt Saddam Hussein were hoping for some sign of disunity in America that might thwart the President's plans regarding Iraq. They found none. The UN vote of Nov. 8 was intimately connected to the US vote of Nov. 5.

As matters moved closer to War, the American Administration moved more and more not unexpectedly toward a position of total unity within its own ranks. The summer rumors, no doubt partly inspired by the summer boredom of the Washington press corps, of a split in the Administration between those advisers led by Secretary Rumsfeld advocating military action and those advisers led by Secretary Powell calling for more diplomacy were put to rest. Secretary Rumsfeld, Vice-President Cheney, and General Powell made it abundantly clear that whatever differences they might have had in the past, by way of effectively advising the Commander in Chief, were by September fully resolved and America was ready to proceed with a united Administration supported rather overwhelmingly by a surprisingly united Congress. Interestingly, public polls consistently throughout the summer and fall of 2002 indicated overwhelming public support for military action against Iraq as long as the White House, the Congress, and the UN were together. As the President moved toward military action that was clearly the case.

The Arab League announced in September that if the US and its Coalition were to move on Iraq they would "open the gates of hell" within the world of Islam. Also in September, most of America's European Allies led by the French and the Germans indicated that although they regarded Saddam to be a threat and a menace they were totally opposed to military action and if the Americans acted alone they would provide no support. China, Japan, Russia and nearly all of America's Allies in the Middle East expressed similar views. In effect, the elites of the world were telling the Americans and the British that they were quite prepared to support America in its War against Osama bin Laden but their endorsement and support did not extend to Saddam Hussein.

By October the situation had changed dramatically. America's European Allies reversed course and offered "limited" support; the Security Council of the UN passed still another resolution calling for Iraqi disarmament but for the first time endorsed a military response should Iraq thwart the will of the Council once again; and America's Middle Eastern Allies tentatively but clearly indicated that the US would be allowed to use bases in Saudi Arabia, Kuwait, and the Gulf States as staging areas for military action.

President Bush by November seemed to have made his decision about the next phase of the War on Terror. America would make a "good faith" effort to calm and encourage its Allies but in the end would move against the Iraqi regime whatever the level of international support or condemnation. The President indicated quite clearly that in the end he believed that public and government support before a War is of little importance—what matters is the level of support one attracts after the campaign. Moreover, the President seemed to conclude that for him the "axis of evil" was an integral part of the world of terrorism. He knew that American military involvement in Iraq would be of a different kind than 1991—this war would be a war to the finish. Saddam and his henchman would be destroyed and the Iraqi regime would be changed and governed from the outside if necessary.

By early October the Pentagon released a communiqué revealing that the battle plans for Target Iraq had been completed. Secretary Rumsfeld set the tone of the moment by commenting that America's military was ready—"we only await the orders of our Commander in Chief." Although the military options before the President were classified and great secrecy was maintained, the general scope of the anticipated action was clear. The US would begin the military operation as it had in Kuwait in 1991 and Kosovo in 1999 with massive aerial assaults designed to "blind" Baghdad from the bulk of its army. The regular Iraqi army divisions in the Western desert would be isolated and no doubt would surrender en masse as they had in 1991. The aerial phase of the operation would be followed by an assault on Baghdad with US and British forces jumping off from Kuwait, Turkey, and the 5th Fleet. The plan was not complicated—Target Iraq would become Target Baghdad. Iraq militarily would be divided into three regions allowing the Kurds of the North and the Shiites of the South to revolt against Iraqi authority while the US and its Allies took control of the Capital.

It did not seem to escape the President's attention that there were substantial risks, particularly to Israel, but also enormous possible gains. Iraq for example is capable of producing five million barrels of oil per day and during the period of the US/UN embargo was producing less than 20 percent of that amount. A friendly Iraq would obviously be moved to a position of full production with the attendant benefits to the West as well as the people of Iraq. The price of gas would go down, the well being of Iraq would go up and other possible antagonists such as the Iranians, the Saudis and the Syrians would go on notice. Also, the President and his spokesmen seemed to understand, indeed even welcomed the possibility that America had embarked upon a regional conflict which might seem frightening at first, but which in the end would provide a vastly improved Middle East from the Western perspective. Secretary Rumsfeld was fond of saying about the Middle East—America must either "get out or get tough." The President had decided not to get out.

It should be noted that one subterranean issue regarding the politics of oil is the difficulty oil has provided for both the West and Islam. Oil has allowed the regimes of the Middle East to live with little taxation and without public representation of any kind within a world of extraordinary wealth. Americans are fond of recalling the Revolutionary code: "no taxation without representation." It may be more revealing for the politics of the Middle East to reverse this concept: no representation without taxation. The anti democratic nature of Muslim politics has been exacerbated radically by the presence of oil—the ability of harsh regimes to flourish in a world requiring no popular participation.

It is also noteworthy to highlight how bizarre and "strange" the politics of oil has worked out. The role of women in the Middle East for example is made unbelievably difficult by the presence of this kind of revenue. Islamic reformers for a very long time have noted that they struggle on in their battles with poverty and despair with half of their populations, women, participating not at all. The politics of oil as we have known it may be coming to an end. American involvement, popular uprisings fueled by population explosions, and Western alternative sources of energy are moving the world into a new and fascinating realm. The Western addiction to cheap oil has forced America and its allies to play in the Middle Eastern quagmire as well as provided a marvelous method of tyranny for ruling Middle Eastern regimes.

Both situations may be changing drastically. Oil has been the culprit—the West for the first time in more than a century seemed to understand that the only "way out" permanently will involve alternative sources of energy. The world of Islam because of contact with the West, declining Western dependence, and internal reform may move in precisely the same direction albeit for entirely different reasons. In short, the status quo in the Middle East will not hold. The Middle East as we have known it is doomed. President Bush seemed bent on shaping events to the Western advantage. Revealingly, his most consistently repeated comment throughout the crisis was that US inaction was the most dangerous and unacceptable option available. Perhaps America's President was following Winston Churchill's thought that when people are fearful about their security they will always prefer a strong leader even if he is occasionally wrong to a weak leader even if he is always correct.

By Christmas 2002, the US/Iraqi confrontation seemed to turn toward its final resolution. On Dec. 7 Baghdad released documents totaling nearly 13,000 pages explaining in baffling and excruciating detail that Iraq had no weapons of mass destruction. The regime asserted that all chemical, biological, and nuclear weapons and programs had been destroyed or discontinued. Furthermore, the Iraqis "welcomed" the more than 200 UN inspectors under the supervision of Hans Blitz who were there to prepare a "final" report for the Security Council. The US and the UK seemed quite satisfied to play out the final round of this curious saga.

Both President Bush and Prime Minister Blair, supported by all of their intelligence and military agencies, maintained quite forcefully that they knew absolutely and without qualification that Iraq had considerable stockpiles of weapons of mass destruction and continued the development of such weapons. In effect, the Americans and their Allies believed that

Iraq was in violation of UN Resolution 1441 the moment the Iraqis released their 13,000 pages of denial. The US continued to move massive numbers of military personnel and resources into the region. By the end of 2002, the "fuse" was lighted. The Iraqis would play for time, disunity in the West, and confusion in the UN. The President would continue on the course he had established quite some time before. The US and its Allies would strike against Iraq and eliminate the regime. The US would pursue its War to "save civilization itself." Few doubted the military outcome.

THE PRELUDE TO WAR

On March 16, 2003 Prime Minister Blair and President George Bush met in the Azores off the coast of Portugal to coordinate their future plans. In a rather extraordinary announcement at the end of the summit, both leaders proclaimed that the United Nations had one more day—24 hours—to either vote that Iraq was in material breach of all previous UN resolutions calling for its disarmament or that Great Britain and the United States in alliance with what they were calling an "Alliance of the willing" would proceed without further UN consultation. The Alliance was made up of 45 nations—the third largest Coalition of nations gathered for war in the history of the world exceeded only by World War II and the Gulf War.

On March 17, 2003 the British Ambassador to the United Nations, Sir Jeremy Greenstock, and the American Ambassador to the United Nations, John Negroponte, announced that the window of diplomacy had closed. Both Ambassadors declared that all further UN activity would be meaningless in light of the fact that one permanent member of the Security Council (France) had declared repeatedly that it would veto any UN Resolution forcing the disarmament of Iraq. The British-American Resolution which would have been the eighteenth UN Resolution calling for Iraqi disarmament and which the British and Americans hoped might bring about some last minute consensus to enforce Resolution 1441, was withdrawn. An emergency meeting of the Security Council for that day was cancelled.

Secretary of State Powell met with the members of the media in New York shortly after the Ambassadors' announcement. The Secretary declared that diplomacy had come to an end. He suggested that Saddam Hussein would be given an ultimatum—flee Iraq or face the wrath of United States and British military action. The news networks of the world announced that the President of the United States would address the nation on the evening of March 17 in what could only be an announcement of war. The bizarre, baffling, and confusing events from the passing of UN Resolution 1441 in November of 2002 to March 17 2003 obviously had come to an end. The Winds of War were at hand—the world awaited military action.

It is important to reflect upon on the events of November to March. UN inspectors had spent a considerable amount of time in Iraq. Dr. Blix announced alternatively that Iraq was not cooperating and that they were cooperatively "splendidly." The Iraqis had managed rather skillfully and not unexpectedly to confuse the inspection process and indeed to play upon the divisions in the West. Secretary Powell's rather remarkable ninety minute "briefing" of the Security Council in February 2003 was initially well received. The Secretary outlined with extraordinary detail and skill the violations he believed the Iraqis continued to carry out in terms of the possession of chemical, bacterial, and nuclear weapons, but Secretary Powell's arguments and the American position proved not to be convincing to the entire Council.

After four months of elaborate and unprecedented diplomacy, the West seemed divided about the Iraqi question. All, at least publicly, agreed that Saddam Hussein was almost entirely an evil creature of politics—all agreed that his regime was a threat to both the Middle East and the world but agreement did not extend to the tactics of how to manage the Iraqi situation. Many UN members led by France and Germany were committed to the idea that more inspections and some form of containment would in the end control Saddam and allow the world to resolve this crisis without military intervention. The US and its Allies obviously believed that containment had not worked and that further delays would only compound the problems of 12 years of "deceit and delay."

In the end, the situation in the UN ended in perhaps the only way it could—the United Nations is not an international organization well suited to decisive action of any kind and certainly not well suited to war-making. Because of the veto the UN normally is reduced to "lowest common denominator" decision-making. It should be noted the UN has only gone to war two times in its long history, Korea in 1950 and the Gulf in 1991, and both wars were primarily US military operations. The UN provided little more than international legitimacy. Perhaps more interesting is the future of the UN particularly in its relationship with the US. President Bush and many others attempted to put the best "spin" on the four months of UN activity preceding the war in Iraq but it was very difficult to imagine an American President in the near future trying again to employ the UN as a basic part of US foreign policy.

American officials noted often before and after March 17 that the UN was not involved in the Serbian war of 1999 primarily because President Clinton knew perfectly well that the UN would never reach agreement on any kind of decisive policy. They observed that the members of the Security Council were forced to bargain for the votes of Angola, Cameroon, Mexico, Guinea, and Chile which had only the most remote interest in the Middle East. Finally, the US Ambassador observed that the moral authority of the UN is always questionable in that a majority of its members represent authoritarian states.

Perhaps more intriguing was the question of why there was such considerable division of opinion in the West. On the eve of war, American public opinion had reached 74 percent calling for an attack on Baghdad while opinion in Western Europe was almost exactly the opposite with at least 74 percent opposing US and allied military operations in the Middle East. Even in Great Britain, the Prime Minister faced considerable opposition to his pro-American stance within his own Labour Party and with the public at large. In March, 111 Labour MPs voted against their own Prime Minister in his call for a Parliamentary Resolution supporting the US-British Alliance. Rather amazingly the Prime Minister carried the day with the support of the opposition Tory Party which supported him almost unanimously. On March 17 in an emergency session of the Cabinet preparing for war, three Ministers including the head of the House of Commons, Robin Cook, resigned in protest. On March 18 the House of Commons supported the Prime Minister's call for war, 412 to 149, but 130 members of the Labour Party revolted against their leader. There were 411 Labour MPs in a House of 659—thus the Prime Minister was able to govern and prevent his Government from "falling" only with the support of the Conservative Party.

The differences no doubt had a great deal to do with the attacks on the United States on Sept. 11, 2001. While Europe, NATO, the EU, and the UN had been very supportive of the US in its hour of need, none experienced first hand the full trauma of these events. Few seemed to pay attention and/or approve of the President's proclamation on Sept. 20, 2001 that terrorists and the states that support them will both be regarded as enemies of the United States. Interestingly, President Bush seemed to be one of the few political leaders in the world who never lost sight of his original declaration. His focus from Sept. 11, 2001 to March 17, 2003 seemed not to waiver at all.

The President was clearly of the view that this heinous and unprecedented attack on the American homeland would not go unanswered and would not be allowed to be the harbinger of even more horrible things to come. George Bush's America would not be deterred by the subleties of diplomacy or the feelings and sensitivities of our Allies while the nation ran the risk of a nuclear or bacterial Pearl Harbor. The world would never again be quite the same for America. The nation itself, to the President, would henceforth be regarded as the frontline of the battle. President Bush's oath of office compelled him to protect the Republic—the destruction of Saddam's Iraq was clearly regarded as part of that oath. The world in the spring of 2003 awaited events to determine the correctness of this view.

Also the crisis provided fertile ground for a difference between France and the United States to surface. President Chirac had long seemed committed to a view of the future concerning which Europe, lead by the EU, which in turn would be led by France, would provide some kind of balancer to a world otherwise dominated by the United States. What was often regarded as anti-Americanism in Europe probably more accurately should be regarded as anti-American domination of international politics. As appealing and perhaps lofty as these sentiments might be, it was perfectly clear in 2003 that any balancer to American power would be far off in the world's future. It is noteworthy that the French announcement that they might initiate a German, Belgian, Russian, French alternative to NATO was generally regarded as bizarre.

Importantly, this French world view was not universally accepted throughout Europe. In what Secretary Rumsfeld had called "old Europe" there was some support for the French —in what might be called "new Europe," that is Eastern Europe and the Baltic, there was practically none. Ten nations of Eastern Europe signed a letter of support for the American President on March 18—all offered to send military assistance. In the final analysis, President Chirac may have turned out to be Prime Minister Blair's and President Bush's "best friend." On the eve of war, British and American public opinion moved sharply toward support for the war. France stood alone, with 45 nations rallying to the British and American banner. Astoundingly, on March 18 President Chirac declared that if Coalition forces were attacked with chemical weapons France in the "spirit of friendship and solidarity" would offer its assistance. The White House responded that the French offer was "notable." When the French foreign minister suggested the same day that France would be willing to help rebuild Iraq after the war, Secretary Rumsfeld commented that "such considerations would of course be up to the new, free Government of Iraq and they might want to remember who had helped them in their hour of need."

CAMPAIGN IRAQ

On the evening of March 17 the President spoke to the nation and the world. The President expressed his views on four subjects related to impending war. First, the President reviewed America's repeated, patient attempts to resolve the crisis with Saddam's regime peacefully. The President noted that Saddam had agreed to the cease-fire of 1991 on the terms that Iraq would destroy all weapons of mass destruction. From that point until March 2003, the US and the UN had sent hundreds of inspectors to Iraq and passed 17 UN resolutions over 12 years calling for the realization of the terms of the original armistice. All failed. The President seemed bent on explaining that the US had gone more than the extra mile for peace and that this war was caused by only one person, the "butcher of Baghdad."

Second, the President outlined his view of the legal basis for American military action. He noted that Congress in October of 2002 had passed overwhelmingly a Resolution in both Houses calling for the Commander in Chief to employ whatever measures might prove necessary to disarm Iraq. Moreover, this Resolution he argued was but a reinforcement of the Resolution of Congress passed overwhelmingly in 1998 during the Clinton Administration calling for the liberation of Iraq. Regime change in Iraq therefore was not a new policy for the US and it was not initiated by President Bush.

Third, the President expressed his disappointment at the inability of the UN to implement its own Resolutions. He added that virtually all of the nations of the world believed that Saddam's Iraq was destabilizing and threatening. In one remark, no doubt directed toward the Republic of France, the President noted that all nations saw the threat and had the same information about Iraq—they did not all have the same resolve. He noted in a most determined way that his Administration had more than enough resolve to proceed to the final solution—he observed "we are peaceful but we are not fragile."

Fourth, President George Bush outlined a theme he seemed most committed to personally and one that marked something of a new departure for American policy in the Middle East. The President suggested that the threat to the West and America was more than real and that the US was not prepared to live with regimes which might carry out a nuclear or bacterial 9/11. He observed that appeasement in the 20th century had led to the holocaust and wars of unimaginable death and destruction but that appeasement of dictators with weapons of mass destruction in the 21st century, might "lead to attacks worse than anything that has ever taken place on this earth."

Finally, the President outlined his vision of the future of Iraq and the Middle East. He noted the tyranny that Iraqis had endured for more than a generation. He observed that "soon the tyrant will be gone." He urged, threatened, and pleaded with the Iraqi military to disobey Saddam and not to give up their lives for a "dying regime." He concluded his rather extraordinary and inspirational remarks with a call for the kind of Iraq that might be possible in the future—a free Iraq that could serve as a beacon of liberty and prosperity for the entire Middle East. He expressed his personal view not often heard within the American elite or within the Middle East—freedom is not a gift given only to America and the West—"freedom is given by God to all of his children." The President seemed more than keen about indicating the moral call to arms which seemed to clearly drive him on. More importantly, the President with few seeming to notice, was transforming almost entirely the basic thrust of US foreign policy. A new call for advancing human rights and providing constitutional government universally, dominated the President's remarks. The Bush Doctrine had come full circle. Human rights and national security were now considered totally intertwined. There would be no victory in the War on Terror without establishing democratic regimes.

The President offered Saddam one last chance to save his life and the lives of his family and the cohort immediately around him. He gave the Iraqi dictator 48 hours to flee the country. The President concluded his remarks on a tone that seemed quite remarkable by the standards of normal Presidential speeches. He was instructing the nation, he was outlining a plan of action, he was reassuring his people, he was calling for a moral crusade, and he was demonstrating his ability to be the commander of America's Armed Forces. President George W. Bush had come a long way from Sept. 11, 2001 to March 17, 2003. He was clearly a confidant, calm, Commander in Chief succeeding in expressing to his nation his ability to govern through this period of considerable uncertainty and fear.

March 19, 2003 at 7:15 pm PDT the President of United States spoke to the nation and to the world. He proclaimed that Operation Iraqi Freedom had begun. After months of diplomacy, the President summarized his war policy rather succinctly: "we will accept no outcome but victory." The President interestingly directed most of his four minute address to the Iraqi people and military. He outlined what they should do: stay in their homes, lay down their arms, and await their liberation.

The first day of battle was what might have been expected, totally unexpected. Instead of America and its Coalition employing what was identified as the "shock and awe" doctrine, the first attacks were quite surgical in nature. Forty cruise and precision missiles were fired on the capital--Baghdad was the region, Saddam Hussein was the target. Three hundred thousand soldiers, six aircraft carriers, 1000 aircraft, and 5000 tanks began to move the battle toward the Iraqi heartland. By day two, the overall strategy was clear. The Coalition would attempt to "decapitate" the regime and hold back the shock attack until political developments were clearer. Within hours, US intelligence reports indicated that Saddam Hussein and senior Iraqi leaders in fact had been hit by the attack of the first night. By day two it was obvious that the Iraqi command and control system was in disarray.

The field operations followed the expected pattern. US and British Special Forces moved into the Iraqi oil fields of the North and South. With the exception of nine oil well fires in the South, the 1900 oil wells of Iraq were almost immediately secured. The 101st Airborne Division moved into the Northern sector of Iraq. The 3rd Infantry Division raced toward Baghdad from its jumping off point in Kuwait. US and Royal Marines captured Basra in the South thus opening a line of supply with the fleet in the Persian Gulf. B1, B2, FA 117 Stealth fighters destroyed all Iraqi air defense systems within the first 24 hours of the war. The "scud box" in Western Iraq was overrun by special operations. By the night of March 20, Iraqi leadership was "blind" and trapped. The Allies raced toward Baghdad. It is noteworthy that no army had moved so much so quickly in the history of warfare.

On March 20 Secretary of Defense Rumsfold indicated that the "shock and awe" strategy which called for a massive attack involving approximately 6000 targets and which the Secretary said would involve force of a "scale and scope never seen before," was being delayed to await political developments in Iraq. Clearly the Allies were hoping for a regime change with as little bloodshed as possible. The entire operation was obviously designed to liberate Iraq—not to destroy it. The initial round of battle was most encouraging—chemical weapons had not been used, Israel was not attacked, the handful of scuds which had been fired were destroyed by Patriot missiles, the oilfields were not destroyed, and all roads were open to the Capital. Perhaps most inspiring was the greeting Allied forces received from most Iraqis they encountered—the Jihad Saddam had proclaimed was replaced by general celebrations that Iraq's deliverance of this incredibly brutal regime was at hand.

The hopes for an almost immediate collapse of the regime were dashed by March 21. The "shock" attack was ordered. One thousand precision weapons were used throughout Iraq—more cruise missiles were fired in ten minutes than had been fired in all of the Gulf War. General Tommy Franks summarized the first five days of the campaign on March 21. First he indicated that all might not go as easily and quickly as many were predicting but the end was not in question. He reviewed the orders he had received from his Commander in Chief: end the regime, destroy Iraq's weapons of mass destruction, destroy terrorists cells and their resources, provide humanitarian relief to the people of Iraq, secure the Iraqi people's greatest asset—the oil fields, and create a transition-representative government. The General assured the world press corps that all these objectives would be accomplished and the campaign was progressing "magnificently."

Interestingly, General Franks indicated the sequences of events that had been followed. In the spirit of employing a strategy of shock, surprise, and flexibility four key moments were noted—D-Day (March 19) which began the campaign with the attempt to destroy senior Iraqi leadership—S-Day (March 19) which involved the deployment of special forces behind Iraqi lines to secure the oil fields and seize the scud box—G-Day (March 20) which started with ground forces pouring across the frontier on their way to Baghdad—and A-Day (March 21) which brought forth the most massive aerial attack every deployed.

By the end of the first week of war, Prime Minister Blair and President Bush met at Camp David. Both leaders publicly reviewed their assessment of the campaign. Both indicated that CentCom's plan was proceeding as scheduled. Both proclaimed that the campaign should be judged not by "timetables but rather by victory." Both noted that the war might be longer than many had originally assumed. Both noted that the "fog of war" would be such that some days would seem very successful and others very painful but the end was totally and absolutely assured. Never to be outdone, Secretary Rumsfeld commented from the Pentagon that Saddam Hussein was a "dead man walking around."

After one week of battle the duration of the campaign was very much in question but the atrocities that might be expected were not. Saddam's regime had been in the business of terrorizing his nation for more than a generation. It seemed to surprise some in the media and the public, but not American leadership, that Iraqi resistance was characterized by extraordinary cruelty. Saddam's forces were divided among the Regular Army (350,000), the Republican Guard (60,000), the Palace Guard (15,000), and the Fedayeen (20,000). The horrifying stories of feigned surrenders, the use of children as human shields, the execution of American and British prisoners of war, the slaughter of innocent Iraqis by Iraqis were carried out almost entirely by the Fedayeen and the Republican Guard. Prime Minister Blair observed that some of the events of the first week revealed a kind of "inhumanity that would horrify anyone with an ounce of decency in their soul."

The Fedayeen had been established in 1995 to provide the regime with death squads organized to roam the countryside and force the population to remain subservient. The Republican and the Palace Guard moved almost entirely into the areas of the Capital and Kirkuk awaiting the final battle of the war. There were scores of intelligence reports indicating that the Republican Guard was prepared to use chemical and bacterial weapons. The President, the Prime Minister and the world awaited events—public opinion in the US and the UK soared toward support for the Coalition efforts. Most seemed to understand that the immediate future might bring horrors of several kinds—most seemed equally convinced of the end result and the just nature of the Coalition cause.

The second week of the War was nothing short of unbelievable. After reports of "pauses," the plan not proceeding properly, and quarrels between the Pentagon and field commanders; events on the battlefield replaced the chatter of TV commentators and "armchair" generals. By April 2 the 101 Airborne Division, the 3rd Armored Division, and the US Marines were within 12 miles of the Iraqi Capital. The same day American troops moved into Najaf near Baghdad. Amazingly, the Grand Ayatollah Sistani, one of the most prominent Shiite clerics in Iraq, issued a Fatwa proclaiming that all Iraqis should cooperate with Coalition forces. The people of Najaf swarmed American troops in a moment of great celebration and relief.

On April 3 Saddam International Airport fell to the Coalition. On April 4 the 3rd Armored Division poured into the Capital itself. Seventeen days of War had produced rather extraordinary results. Most of Iraq was under Coalition control, organized resistance was gone, most of the regular Iraqi Army had faded back into the population, the horrors of chemical attack had been avoided, Israel had not been attacked, Kuwait had suffered no damage from scud attacks, the international airport was lost, and the Capital was under siege. The War plan had five parts—general buildup and deployment, preparation of the battlefield, the three hundred and fifty mile race to Baghdad, control of the Capital, and the total elimination of the regime of Saddam Hussein. In seventeen days, the Coalition had completed the first three parts and was swarming the Capital.

The seventeen days of March and April very likely will be remembered as among the most remarkable days in the history of warfare. Coalition forces had moved almost half way around the world and with fewer than 100 combat deaths were on the brink of annihilating the Iraqi regime. The extraordinary, fascinating, and unprecedented television coverage had provided glimpses into war never seen before but it had also confused the situation. Television audiences were watching the incidents of war highlighted by relatively unimportant firefights—what they did not see was the quite unbelievable effectiveness of the special operations and the aerial campaign. Special Forces had moved throughout Iraq for months and the aerial campaign was highlighted by the use of more than 23,000 precision weapons, 750 Tomahawk cruise missiles, and 21,000 "strike sorties." The dramatic scene of an American army moving into the Capital on April 4 was in the end less important than the fact that the four Republican Guard Divisions deployed to defend Baghdad were gone—some had fled, some surrendered, some died—but all were gone.

The news from the War on April 8, 2003 was nothing short of astounding. At approximately 2 pm, Baghdad time, an American B-1 bomber, guided by "very reliable" intelligence reports, fired four precision 2000-pound bombs on a residential district of Baghdad. Pentagon officials confirmed that the target was Saddam Hussein, his two sons, and other high-ranking Iraqi leaders. Although the attack was not successful, the long nightmare of politics in Iraq had come to an end. The Iraqi elite had nowhere to hide. Rumors of Saddam's death of course did not bring forth immediate peace nor did Madisonian democracy break out throughout the Middle East, but one B-1 bomber and the sixty foot crater left in its wake had demonstrated that there are occasions in history when single events dramatically bring forth extraordinary changes. The people of Iraq awaited their deliverance—the people of the entire region anticipated a "new day" in the politics of the Middle East.

It is also vital to note that April 8 marked the first of some discoveries of weapons of mass destruction. The 101st Airborne Division captured a factory with "significant" amounts of weaponized nerve gas. The cache of tabun and sarin was precisely what Secretary Powell had told the UN would be found throughout Saddam's regime—the same weapons the UN had failed to uncover in 12 years of inspections. Nevertheless, American forces did not discover stockpiles of weapons of mass destruction. Few believed Saddam Hussein voluntarily destroyed these weapons and even more improbably had refused to cooperate with the UN and destroyed his regime because he refused to demonstrate to the US where the weapons had gone. It may never be completely clear where the missing weapons went.

The War against Saddam did not have an official end—few had expected it would. No government surrendered, no leader tendered his sword, no bands played—the nature of 21st century war against terrorist and rogue regimes was at hand. But April 9 did mark a symbolic end to the War. At 6:50 am Baghdad time, the largest statute of Saddam Hussein in the Government District of Baghdad was brought down by the citizens of Iraq with the assistance of US Marines. The forty foot bronze edifice of Saddam seemed to symbolize the entire regime, the entire nightmare of a generation of indescribable tyranny.

As the statute crashed to the ground, tens of thousands of the citizens of Baghdad poured into the streets waving American flags and chanting "George Bush, George Bush." The War that had so divided the United Nations and Western Europe took on a new clarity. The citizens of Iraq voted with their celebrations throughout the nation. On April 10 the Northern cities, the last holdouts of the regime, experienced similar public demonstrations and outbursts of great emotion. On that day Iraq's Ambassador to the United Nations left with his entire delegation—he proclaimed: "the game is over, it is all over." Interestingly, the Iraqi delegation fled to France.

By mid April the battle for Iraq was officially over. On May 1 President Bush spoke from the deck of the USS Abraham Lincoln in San Diego proclaiming that hostilities had come to an end. He concluded his address to the nation by quoting the prophet Isaiah: "To the captives, 'Come out,' – and to those in darkness, 'Be Free.'" The difficult task of rebuilding a civil society was started. Iraq was divided into British, Polish, and American sectors. Several European nations dispatched troops to reinforce the British and Polish deployment. The UN participated in humanitarian efforts but was not involved in the political administration of Iraq. The outcome was very much in doubt but a great deal had been accomplished in a remarkably short period of time.

On December 13, 2003, Task Force 21 of the 4th Infantry Division captured Saddam Hussein in Ad Dawr near Tikrit, Iraq. Saddam was hiding in a "spider hole" buried with nearly one million US dollars. Six hundred American Special Forces were part of the raid. US soldiers were forced to dig the "butcher of Baghdad" out of his hiding spot. The Iraqi dictator, who had ordered so many to their deaths, had called for so many

Jihads, and had paid for so many children to do his dying for him as suicide-bombers, did not resist—not a shot was fired. With one of Saddam's palaces in sight, Coalition troops pulled a filthy, beaten Saddam from his hole in the cellar of a dirt hut. The first US soldier who encountered the Iraqi dictator said: "we bring regards from President Bush." Saddam pleaded: "don't shoot me."

This amazingly ignominious end to Saddam's freedom marked a turning point in the reconstruction of Iraq and had enormously important consequences for the entire region. Millions of Iraqis poured into the streets of the nation in a celebration some had awaited since 1979. The Baathist resistance no longer had a leader. Those who feared that Saddam, who had escaped the Americans in 1991 and again in early 2003, might return to power under some extraordinary set of circumstances, no longer had to worry about such dire developments. It is important to note that Saddam's sons, Uday and Cusay, were killed by Coalition forces in July 2003. The "lineage of evil" was broken forever.

The 35 years of Iraq's long, long nightmare with tyranny and mass murder involving the execution of nearly one million innocent Iraqi men, women, and children mercifully came to a close by Christmas 2003. The Iraqi Governing Council vowed to try Saddam in the full view of world opinion to review the unbelievably nightmarish nature of his regime. President Bush in his address to the nation on December 14 proclaimed that the Iraqi nightmare of living with torture chambers and mass murders was over. Prime Minister Blair said with perfect English understatement: "Saddam is gone from power—he will not be back." Even President Chirac felt compelled to join the euphoria of the moment with his comment: "France is delighted—the democratization of Iraq is assured."

Iraqi elections were held in January 2005 creating a national assembly empowered to write a national constitution. The transfer of sovereignty from the Coalition to an Iraqi national government was completed on June 30, 2004. The new Iraqi constitution was approved in a national election on October 15th. Full elections for an Iraqi parliament were held December 15th, 2005. Few expected that the struggle for democracy in Iraq would proceed easily. The US had lost 3000 military personnel in the Iraqi war by the end of 2006. Several American civilians were brutally murdered by the terrorists but most observers believed by the fall of 2006 that the task was at least possible and would have an amazingly positive if not chilling effect on other regimes in the area. Indeed Coalition success in Iraq might bring forth what President Bush and Prime Minister Blair had discussed so often—the beginning of a new Golden Age of freedom for the world generally and the Middle East specifically. The Iraqi elections of 2005 brought forth the greatest hope. Twelve million Iraqis voted in the nation's first free election. By September 2005, a new Iraqi government was functioning reasonably well. Iraqi security forces were gradually replacing Coalition forces in the struggle to maintain order. By the fall of 2005, Iraq's new President proclaimed that US and Coalition forces should expect to withdraw from Iraq entirely during 2006. Interestingly, the new government of Iraq was made up of a Kurdish president, Jalal Talabani; a Sunni speaker of the parliament, Hajim al-Hassani, and a Shi'a prime minister, Ibrahim al-Jaafari.

The relationship between the Iraqi invasion and America's overall war strategy became the center of considerable national debate. According to the President and all of his advisers including Secretaries Powell, Rumsfeld, and Dr. Rice; Iraq was a threat to the United States because it had supported terrorist groups such as Hamas and Hizballah and had given various forms of support to Al Qaeda. More to the point of the timing of the invasion, Saddam's regime was seen as a growing menace that would ultimately endanger America's Allies in the Middle East and Europe.

The Administrations position however controversial was clear. Saddam's Iraq was part of a global terrorist threat to the security of the US and its Allies. Saddam's Iraq would only grow more dangerous. Saddam's Iraq could not be controlled by the UN. The global, US policy of "containing" Saddam had failed and immediate military action was required.

The greatest danger, according to the America position, involved Saddam's weapons of mass destruction. Saddam had used WMD in the past, virtually all Western Intelligence sources believed he still possessed WMD, and the President argued that he would definitely acquire more and more threatening weapons in the future including nuclear weapons.

Once victory had been achieved and the Coalition did not find what most observers expected—massive numbers of WMD, it immediately became apparent that there would be great controversy about the "missing" weapons. To some critics of the Administration, the entire justification of the war was lost and the military campaign was illegitimate.

Most observers, however, believed the intelligence used by the Americans was flawed but not by conspiracy rather because of the nature of the espionage itself. As Director Tenet stated over and over again: intelligence gathering is not a perfect science. Moreover, in the final analysis the "missing" weapons were irrelevant. Once the war started they became unimportant. Interestingly, according to President Bush and his Democratic opponent for the White House, Senator Kerry: failure in Iraq was no longer an option. Therefore, whatever the cause of the war, Coalition failure in Iraq would lead to a profound victory for the terrorists and would truly endanger the US and its Allies. The WMD debate concerning the war, therefore, was fascinating history but it was no longer vital to the debate regarding America's options for the future.

The US national debate about Iraq intensified in 2006. The midterm elections of 2006 and the Presidential election of 2008 were no doubt on the minds of American politicians. The general tone of the debate, however, remained fairly constant. Many Democrats focused on the missing weapons of mass destruction, some suggested the President had lied and rigged the case for war, and a few even called for an immediate withdrawal from Iraq. The vast majority of American political leaders, however, were more interested in the debate about how to succeed in Iraq. Most were not tempted by calls for withdrawal. Interestingly , both Senators Clinton and McCain proclaimed that failure in Iraq would embolden the terrorists and threaten the American homeland itself. The Presidential campaign for 2008 started the moment the midterm of elections of 2006 were completed. Clearly Iraq would be at the center of the campaign. What is not clear as of this writing is whether the major contenders will remain committed to victory in Iraq or whether the major parties will break into a pro-war, anti-war division.

The US military had demonstrated once again America's utterly dominant military position in world affairs. Saddam Hussein's regime was gone. Human rights in Iraq and the Middle East had been advanced. Syria, Iran, and North Korea not surprisingly became extremely "reasonable" in their approach to the United States. Finally, as former Secretary of State Henry Kissinger proclaimed, the War against terror and the war against rogue states was being won. He added that he had never in his life been so proud to be an American. America would probably never be quite the same after Sept. 11, 2001. America's age of innocence was no doubt gone forever, but the terrorists had done something they could not have imagined in their worst nightmares—in the spirit of Admiral Yamamoto's declaration after Pearl Harbor—they had "aroused a sleeping giant."

PART IV
CONCLUSION

LESSONS FROM THE PAST

The War on Terrorism has all the appearances of being something totally new in the world of international politics. In many ways that may be true. But rarely is anything in the affairs of nations entirely new. There are, no doubt, many lessons, at least at the operational level, from America's past which will serve us well in the confusing future we face.

World War II ended in Europe in May 1945 with the collapse of the Nazi empire. The following August the Empire of Japan surrendered following the atomic attacks on Hiroshima and Nagasaki. The world's most horrifying experience, involving more than 50 million deaths, came to an end with an extraordinary note of hope. There was global anticipation that this nightmare would finally bring to the world some drastic alteration in international politics that would end war as we had known it. World War I had failed to be the war that would "end all wars" but many believed World War II would accomplish that objective.

Tragically the "dreams of 1945" were almost immediately dashed. The Cold War replaced World War II as the new crisis of international affairs. The Cold War in some ways was even more frightening. It was a war fought on a global scale between two imperial giants both armed with nuclear weapons and both surrounded by scores of Allies. The Cold War lasted approximately 50 years—20 million people died in the wars of the Cold War. It cost the US about $13 trillion. For the Soviets the cost was total—the USSR collapsed on Christmas day 1991. Soviet Communism's 84-year struggle, which had started in 1917 with the Bolshevik Revolution, ended in total, absolute failure. This nightmarish experiment in politics mercifully came to an end but not before the "evil empire" had terrorized the world and its own population.

The Cold War was caused more than anything else by Soviet aggression. Although Western academics argued for decades about the real cause of the conflict, all of the debates now seem quite peculiar and pointless. Perhaps Mikhail Gorbachev is the best, most neutral source. Former President Gorbachev suggests that most of Soviet history involved a criminal regime bent on world dominion.

In 1945 the Soviet Army, as a result of World War II, was in control of Eastern Europe. The six nations of that region—Bulgaria, Rumania, Czechoslovakia, Hungary, East Germany, and Poland—with 124 million people became part of a Soviet imperial system of satellites. The Baltic countries—Latvia, Estonia, and Lithuania—with 24 million people suffered the same fate. Ironically World War II had started in Poland over the question of Polish freedom. Poland and Eastern Europe in 1945 traded one form of horrifying tyranny, Nazism, with another, Soviet Communism.

Moreover, Stalin's Russia was on the move in other areas. The Soviets refused in 1945 to leave Iran with the ominous prospect of moving toward the Gulf. The Soviets encouraged French and Italian Communists to seize power. Stalin's operatives promoted civil war in Greece and Turkey. In 1950 Stalin promoted, perhaps inspired the North Korean invasion of South Korea. Quite independently of the Soviets, Mao's Communist forces seized power in Beijing in Oct. 1949. By the summer of 1950 it was clear that America and the West faced a threat of monumental consequences. America at the end of World War II had done what it always does in war—it returned as quickly as possible to the American island. America demobilized roughly 12 million men and women from the Armed Forces and settled in for what it assumed would be a return to "normalcy."

Harry S. Truman assumed the Presidency in April of 1945. Harry Truman by all calculations should have been a mediocre to horrible president. It is still not clear why Franklin Roosevelt even selected him to be his fourth Vice-President. Truman had been Vice-President for less than six weeks when FDR died on April 12. Perhaps the old expression is true that "God takes care of fools, drunks and the United States of America." President Truman became a giant among Presidents—a towering figure of the 20th century. Truman will always be remembered for his bizarre election victory of 1948, his rather peculiar way of communicating, and his decision to use the atomic bomb but his most extraordinary contribution to history involves none of these things. It was his authorship of America's response to the Cold War.

Truman from 1945 to 1950 moved the United States from its return to normalcy and its return to isolationism to a policy that came to be known of as containment. Containment involved containing Communism—primarily Soviet Communism. Containment had two primary components—one economic and one military. Economically the US became committed to the restoration of Europe and Japan economically through the Marshall Plan and other programs of foreign assistance.

Militarily the US created the NATO Alliance in 1949 followed thereafter by other multilateral alliance systems such as SEATO, CENTO, and the RIO Pact all designed to draw a military line of containment around world Communism. It should be noted that containment was not a policy calling for victory—containment involved containment putting off questions of victory for another day. Containment did, however, commit the US to massive peacetime alliances overseas for the first time in American history. Truman's containment was a call to arms and call to permanent involvement with the world. It marked what many hoped would be the end of American isolationism forever.

In grand geopolitical terms the next great moment of the Cold War involved the alterations in US policy brought about by President Nixon and Secretary of State Henry Kissinger from 1969 to 1974. According to President Nixon, the world had undergone rather fundamental changes by 1969 and containment would have to be revised. The Nixon Doctrine or the Nixon view of international politics was based on the following calculations: the world Communist movement was fragmenting, ideology or the "isms" were losing their importance in the world, China was emerging as a completely independent political force, the Soviets had "caught" the Americans in the nuclear arms race, and Less Developed Countries were declining in importance. The President and the Secretary dreamed of a new structure of peace brought about by the US adjusting its policies to the new international reality.

Nixon's policies came to be called the policies of détente. Détente is a French word, which means very little in French and almost nothing in English. In reality détente meant "improved relations with the Soviet Union." The benign part of détente was that it was time to do business with the Communists—time to learn to live with the Communists—time to do more than just contain our adversaries. The more Machiavellian part of détente was the President's view that fragmentation in the world of Communism allowed the US an opening in international politics that would benefit both the US and the world.

The actual policies that flowed from these calculations revolved around President's Nixon extraordinary trip to China in February of 1972. From 1969 to 1972, the US had moved with absolute secrecy toward an opening with China. The great anti-communist Nixon who was regarded as one of the leaders of the Taiwan Lobby was moving America toward normalizing relations with Mao's China. The outward appearance of the trip seemed to be the desire to establish relations with China, allow China to join the UN, and allow the US and China to begin economic and cultural exchanges. The world press tagged all of this "ping pong diplomacy." The reality of the situation was quite different. The President wanted from China a hammer to use against the Soviets. As he so often explained to the White House Staff: "the China game will make the Soviet game work and the Soviet game will make the China game work."

By 1972 America's policy of containment had been changed to a policy of triangular diplomacy among the three giants of world politics—China, America, and Russia. The US wanted to get out of Vietnam and viewed the road out of Vietnam to run through Beijing and Moscow. The US also wanted to avoid war between China and Russia, which had already started along the Amur River. President Nixon was convinced that a Russo-Chinese war would involve nuclear weapons and would unleash on the world forces that might become totally uncontrollable. Of course ping-pong matches, trade, and cultural exchanges would be nice but all such things were regarded as totally marginal. America was actively trying to change the entire international system.

The Chinese viewed the triangle as essential to their interests. They wanted American assurances that the US would help them if the Soviets moved toward hegemony in Asia. The assurances were given. The Soviets viewed the triangle as essential but of course for entirely different reasons. The USSR wanted very much to deal with Nixon to avoid a Sino-American alliance, to make a deal regarding nuclear weapons thus allowing them to reduce defense expenditures, and to create a system of trade that would allow them to buy their way out of their domestic economic woes.

Nixon's détente worked. Old adversaries did not become friends but did learn how to negotiate their way to better relations. China avoided war with Russia, America got out of Vietnam, and an entirely new relationship was forged between the US and the USSR. The relationships were highlighted by the Shanghai Communiqué of February 1972 and the Moscow summit of May 1972.

The next grand moment of the Cold War involved the election of Governor Reagan to the Presidency. President Reagan was perhaps the most popular, least understood of the modern Presidents. President Reagan was a peculiarly uncomplicated individual. He was more than anything else a romantic and a revolutionary which probably more than anything else explained his amazing popularity. He was of course remarkably gifted as a communicator, which made all of his tasks easier. Winston Churchill may have been correct that a leader's greatest power comes from oration. President Reagan worked for and dreamed of two things above all else. He was interested in reducing taxes and regulations in the American system thereby, as he was fond of telling all who would listen, "getting the government off the backs of the America people." But more than anything else he was going to single-handedly, with or without political council, rid the world of Communism and nuclear weapons.

Reagan's methods were almost as surprising as Nixon's had been. He immediately set out to "rearm" America nearly doubling the defense budget in two years. He tagged the Soviet Union as the "Evil Empire" signaling to many a new era of hostility with the USSR. He pursued policies from Afghanistan to Angola designed to overthrow communist regimes. Finally, and what appeared to be totally contradictory, he called for a new era of cooperation with the Soviet Union particularly focusing on nuclear arms control.

President Reagan met President Gorbachev at the summit in Switzerland in 1985. Astoundingly the man who was trying to save Communism and the man who was trying to destroy it almost immediately were able to communicate. Gorbachev has said: "I liked Ronald Reagan from the beginning" and knew we could in the end do business with him. Gorbachev knew Reagan was an adversary but an adversary who was predictable and honorable. Presidents Reagan and Gorbachev met at the summit in 1985, 86, 87, and 88. When they were done they had changed the world—they had become co-authors to the end of the Cold War.

In an oversimplified but still important way, there would seem to be three methods of diplomacy, three models of foreign policy that emerged from America's Cold War experience. All three may form the debate that is sure to come in the War on Terrorism. In a very preliminary way, all are already present. Put in the form of questions: should we learn in the spirit of President Truman how to contain the terrorists? Containment would allow us to stop the threat now and await the day when events within the enemy camp will solve many problems we do not have to directly confront now.

In a very real way, the US followed a policy of containment toward Saddam Hussein hoping that either he would die or be removed by a coup and replaced by more benign leadership. The argument for containment is simple—it is easier and perhaps less dangerous than other options. The argument against it is also simple—in the end we may contain too long, we may be containing our enemies just at the moment they strike perhaps with incalculable damage from bioterrorism or nuclear weapons. The critics of containment believe the historical analogy one needs is the Nazis not the Soviets. We could not have contained the Third Reich.

Should we learn from President Nixon in the spirit of détente how to do business with our adversaries albeit always playing one off against the other? Should we learn from Disraeli, Richelieu and all the advocates of realpolitik that although containment will not work, grand schemes of victory might be equally futile?

Should we learn from President Reagan that in the end the world's greatest democracy should save the day by advocating more democracy? Perhaps Iran is the key. It is certainly true that the vast majority of young Iranians are essentially pro-American. They have experienced and rejected the kind of regime the extremists are advocating. There are other rumblings for democratic reform in the Arab/Muslim world from Turkey, Jordan, Egypt, the UAE, and Saudi Arabia. Freedom is our natural ideology and our natural ally—we should liberate the "Arab street." The argument for democratic reform is obvious—the West is always comfortable with such calls to battle. The argument against this approach is tremendously complicated but comes down to concerns it simply will not work and such policies might unleash forces in the Middle East we could never control—in the end we might destroy our Allies and play directly into the hands of the radicals. The future of a liberated Iraq may be the key. I am not confident which of the lessons of the past might serve America and its Coalition Allies the best. No doubt the future will be predictably more complicated than we would like. Perhaps shades of all three will be useful—perhaps none. I am, however, confident that the Cold War policies of the past 50 years will form the national debate if for no other reason than policy-makers and academics normally argue by analogy. At least we should prepare ourselves for the debate by knowing the history involved. It is, however, essential to note that President Bush and Prime Minister Blair had no confusion about their choice – Western survival is totally dependent on advancing democratic values.

REALPOLITIK REVISITED

General Powell stated on Oct. 18, 2001 during the President's summit in China: "not only is the Cold War over, the post Cold War is over." The War on Terrorism may in the end be most important in that it will mark a drastic, dramatic change in the nature of international politics. Professor Richard Rosecrance has observed that international politics is often characterized by different international systems. International systems he argues are "styles of diplomacy." From the Treaty of Westphalia in 1648 to 2004, international politics has been dominated by nation-states but the styles of diplomacy have changed often.

Normally the numbers of great powers are the clue—a world dominated by one power is called unipolar, a world of two great powers is thought of as bipolar, a world of many great nations is multipolar. A unipolar world is characterized by imperial dominance, a bipolar world by the "zero-sum" game, and a multipolar world by constantly changing alliances. International systems also are influenced by ideas. The world of the 19th century involved notions of imperial conquest often accompanied by dreams of Westernizing or "civilizing the barbarians." The world of the 20th century was nearly destroyed by ideological conflicts—wars between the totalitarians and the constitutional democrats. The world of the 21st century seems destined to be a world consumed by religious conflict.

Sept. 11 may be regarded historically as changing traditional views of international politics. Before Sept. 11 most scholars were confidant that much of the 21st century would be a unipolar world dominated by America. Sometime before the end of the 21st century, unipolarity would be replaced by multipolarity not because America would have failed but because several other centers of power such as Europe and Japan would have caught the Americans. All of this may still come to pass but Sept. 11 has introduced several astounding, unexpected twists and turns in the affairs of nations.

Perhaps the most amazing development of the autumn of 2001 was the new relationship that developed between Russia and America. President Putin and President Bush quite remarkably began to refer to one another as close friends. Six summits took place from 2001 to 2006. More importantly, American policy toward Russia and Russia's response turned the relationship entirely around. Gone were the days of quarreling about NATO expansion, indeed Russia became in effect the 20th member of NATO in June of 2002. Gone were the days of focusing on the ABM treaty of 1972, gone were the days of America defending the Chechnyan rebels, and gone were the days of Russia's visceral reaction to the construction of a US missile defense system. Remarkably, America's official withdrawal from the ABM Treaty in December of 2001 brought forth only a Russian note of "disappointment."

The former Cold War adversaries seemed to have come full circle— a coincidence of interest had replaced 80 years of hatred and fear. President Putin seemed convinced that Russia, which no doubt has the worst geopolitical position on earth, and constantly worries about the disintegration of the entire Federation could use a new, powerful friend. The US rather quickly and one would think wisely seemed intent upon finding a new and potentially powerful friend in its War on Terrorism. Interestingly, Washington became wildly involved in Russian energy resources as a part of its long-range vision of the future of the West. It is also somewhat beyond the unbelievable that Russia in November 2001 seemed delighted to allow the US military to use its airspace and the bases of former Republics to launch military assaults against Afghanistan. Even Russian quarrels with the US about Operation Iraqi Freedom seemed not to threaten the overall American/Russian relationship.

America's new relationship with Russia will be only the first of several astounding changes in the style of diplomacy. America's difficulties with China seemed suddenly to have little importance. Taiwan, missile defense, and Chinese defense spending were barely mentioned at the Shanghai summit of 2001. President Bush's visit to China in 2005 was marked by an almost peculiar level of friendliness. North Korea and trade were the major points of discussion not the quarrels of an earlier time. Old enemies may become new friends—old friends may become adversaries. Constantly shifting alliances will no doubt be the order of the day. The days of Metternich, Disraeli, and Nixon are back. The greatest issue may be whether the West is up to the confusing nature of the task. Americans for 225 hundred years have wrestled with two questions regarding world affairs—"should we get involved and should we support primarily regimes which promote democratic values." Americans have normally answered the first question with a resounding "no" and the second with a more cautious "yes."

Neither question will serve the nation during the War against Terrorism. America will be involved in world affairs for as long as the mind can reach or it will be destroyed. The issue of democratic politics will be painfully confusing. Some of our Allies in the new War will be democracies—many will not. Perhaps the most frightening realization to the West may be that it is quite possible Osama bin Laden, until recently, was the most popular, respected leader in the world of Islam. Perhaps we will have to take counsel in Winston Churchill's comment of 1941 during Operation Barbarossa—"if Hitler invaded Hell itself I would find a kind word for the Devil." Regarding the America-British alliance with Stalin, Churchill added: "I would make a deal with the Devil himself to defeat Herr Hitler—and I believe I just did."

WHAT WILL BE NEXT

After nearly five years of war, America and its Allies had notched up some important successes against the dark and sinister forces which destroyed the twin towers. Led by an extraordinarily determined and effective President; the regime which sponsored Al Qaeda was toppled, Al Qaeda and its off shoots were on the run, the paymasters of terrorism had been targeted worldwide, America's Coalition successfully destroyed the regime of Saddam Hussein, al-Zargawi was killed by US forces, the people of Iraq had established the beginning forms of democratic state, America's national security doctrine was refocused on preemptive strikes, and the US had begun the agonizing task of constructing a frontline system of homeland defense. Recalling another dark moment in the history of Western Civilization, it seemed obvious that there would be many setbacks ahead—more terror, more death to innocent civilians, and more attacks on the American homeland—clearly "the beginning of the end" was not at hand but also rather clearly "the end of the beginning" had been achieved.

It is important to note, and no doubt frightening to consider for America's adversaries, that the United States in less than 12 years had dispatched its military forces to Kuwait, Kosovo, Afghanistan, and Iraq. All four campaigns, in four of the most difficult possible places for the extension of American power, were won in unprecedented, extraordinary ways. A new order of politics and military power was clearly at hand. Never in the history of nations had one nation reached such military superiority in relationship to the rest of the world. All four campaigns involved a total of about 300 combat deaths—allied armies totaling over a million soldiers had fought brilliantly, bravely, and successfully sustaining virtually "no losses."

American wars had brought a new look to international politics. Henceforth, when there is a crisis in the world the first question all will ask is "what is the American position?" American wars do not involve wondering who will win—that is known before the battle starts. The issue before the world is where will America choose to use its power? Even more important, to what political ends will the United States exercise military power? Will America be driven by attempts to be the "balancer" in world affairs or will it be more dedicated to throwing aside the status quo and advancing the cause of human freedom? Neoconservatives see these goals as the same. They probably are not but there is no doubt merit in the view that free nations will never be secure until all of the key players in international politics are free as well.

Most reasonable observers seem to know that the United States is almost by instinct an isolationist nation—it exercises power reluctantly and becomes easily obsessed by calculations about when the nation can "bring the boys home." America's role as the world's balancer and the beacon of extending liberty and civility internationally may be an exhilarating thought for many across the seas but it is a role the Americans will always find difficult. Perhaps the most important international question of the 21st century will not involve when the United States chooses to become involved, but for how long?

As the Presidential campaign of 2004 reached full stride, several disturbing and familiar developments were clear. The Democratic Party, as reflected by the nine Democrats running for President, had moved to a position of becoming the anti-war party. Although this policy seemed somewhat incoherent in that most of the nine had initially supported American military efforts in Afghanistan and Iraq and most supported the reconstruction efforts of Afghanistan and Iraq, the "loyal opposition" nevertheless cast its opposition in vague and vitriolic anti-war attacks on the President. By the spring of 2004, Senator John Kerry of Massachusetts had emerged as the Democratic nominee. Kerry criticized the President stridently about Iraqi policy but did not advocate withdrawal. His awkward position was reflected by the fact that the Senator had voted for the Senate resolution on Iraq but voted against the funds to support the war. In effect Senator Kerry became a pro-war candidate leading an anti-war party. His selection of Senator John Edwards of North Carolina as his running mate was no doubt an attempt to appeal to independent voters but the Democratic nominee's dilemma continued through the campaign.

All of this may be explained by the simple calculation that President Bush was the kind of presidential candidate who would be extremely difficult to defeat. He was well-liked as an individual, he was regarded almost universally as a political leader of considerable integrity, his political base was secure, he had no opposition within the Republican Party, he had almost unlimited campaign funds, he had considerable appeal to moderates and Reagan democrats, he had realized great success as a Commander in Chief, the economy was robustly rebounding, and he was surrounded by controversial but unquestionably qualified lieutenants. The Democratic opposition no doubt came to the conclusion that they had to challenge the President on his war policy or they would face certain defeat.

The great problem with this approach is that it came dangerously close to putting partisanship above national interest. It has long been regarded in America as honorable and worthwhile to be a member of a political party—partisan loyalty is essential to the civic culture but it has also long been assumed that partisanship is intolerable when it replaces concerns for the interests of the nation. America's policy in the Middle East and indeed its policies generally regarding the global War on Terror, were to a substantial degree dependent on the world assuming the nation would remain united in its efforts. Would America, in the words of the President, "stay the course?"

But there was no doubt more at play than just the partisan lust for power. All of this has to be cast in the light of America's long standing "commitment" and natural affinity to isolationism. Isolationism nearly destroyed the Republic in the 1930s and led to perhaps the most disgraceful moment in the history of the nation. Isolationism comes easily to the American people—the Revolutionary tradition and America's extraordinarily beneficial geopolitical position constantly fuel it.

Partisanship and isolationism also are reinforced by a free but sometimes irresponsible press. The American press is driven by the legacies of Watergate and Monicagate as well as 24 hour news "shows" which find good news intolerable and bad news exhilarating. Long gone were the days of General Eisenhower and the American press corps of World War II. The press is clearly uncomfortable with its role as an essential partner with the government in the War on Terror.

More American policeman died on the streets of America from May 1, 2003 to September, 2006 than American soldiers died in Operation Iraqi Freedom and the reconstruction of Iraq. But each soldier's tragic death was reported as if it represented a failure in national policy. Tragic incidents such as the abuse of Iraqi prisoners at Abu Gharib became full "feeding frenzies" in the US press. Little was reported about the reconstruction of Iraq. Even less about the US and Coalition plan to move from an occupation appointed governing council to the creation of a constitution followed by elections. Little was reported about the extraordinarily successful reconstruction of Iraqi schools, banks, hospitals, factories, oil refineries, and hydroelectric systems. Almost nothing was reported about how inconceivably horrible it would be to return Iraq to the hands of Saddam Hussein or some other psychopathic killer. Rarely was there any serious discussion of what kind of Dark Age would descend on the Middle East and how "thrilled" the forces of global terror would be if America and its Allies failed in their efforts.

2007 had all the markings of a fatal year for American foreign policy. If the nation, for whatever combination of reasons, moved toward withdrawal from the Middle East and rejection of the Bush Doctrine, the War on Terror might take a very dark and fateful turn. The American people would have to decide, as all great imperial people must ultimately decide, whether or not their mission was worthwhile—specifically whether or not the President's view that the War on Terror should be fought on the frontlines of the battle destroying both home-bases and sponsoring-bases for the terrorists or whether America should retreat to the comfortable but perhaps terribly dangerous position of hiding on its island hoping that prayer, the UN, and diplomacy would protect the Republic.

America's ancient demons—isolationism, partisanship, and a biased press were loose. Would they be controlled by great political leadership and a wise people? Would bipartisanship replace the petty desire for securing political power? Would the "shining city on the hill" fulfill its destiny and remain the world's beacon of hope? Would human freedom replace barbarism and tyranny in international politics? Would America reach for the stars and realize its destiny? Throughout 2006 the world awaited America's answers. The presidential campaign of 2004 provided a limited indication of America's decision. Although there was considerable confusion and concern about the American occupation of Iraq, both presidential candidates supported victory in Iraq without qualification. President Bush's rather substantial victory reinforced the view that America would "stay the course." Campaign 2004 was more about the war than anything else. The President won 51 percent of the vote and 30 states. Clearly the nation was worried about the war but reluctantly had voted for victory in Iraq. America's Global War on Terror would be defined by President Bush – it would be a war against both the terrorists and regimes which support terrorism. But America's support for the war continued to decline in 2006. The President's once extraordinary approval ratings had dropped to almost 30 percent. America's "staying power" became even more questionable with the midterm elections of 2006. The presidential election of 2008 would probably prove decisive. Interestingly, the leading Democratic candidate called for withdrawal while the leading Republican candidate called for more troops to be sent to Iraq. A great deal would also depend on events in Iraq.

Although it will no doubt be true that the world's War on Terrorism will last for a very long time, it was not true that some sense of victory would take the same length of time. The keys to victory were fairly clear—Osama bin Laden and Saddam Hussein had to be removed from international politics. That was accomplished in 2003. The home bases for terrorism, meaning nations, must never be allowed to function with immunity. That goal seemed within reach by the end of 2006. Finally, America's commitment to Arabian affairs may be the final determinant of victory. If America goes to the Middle East as it did to Europe in 1947 with the Marshall Plan and NATO—goes to the Middle East to stay—goes to the Middle East to win the battle against the slaughtering of innocent civilians and to advance human rights—America and its Coalition will no doubt be victorious. The war will be won. President George W. Bush will be correct—civilization will prevail.

At an even grander level of policy, President Bush had since September 11, 2001 drastically changed the entire thrust of the US foreign policy. Leaving aside the debate about the correctness of his views, the President had moved the nation from the politics of containment, detente, and realpolitik to a global commitment to human rights and democracy. George Bush's view of international relations, as indicated in his inaugural address of 2005, was not difficult to identify. Freedom and peace were synonymous. There would be no enduring peace for America and no final victory over terrorism until all the key players in global politics are democratic regimes.

EPILOGUE

The emotion of the moment is such that it seems appropriate to end this presentation with a personal note. I searched my soul to find the one thing I have done in my career, which might capture my thoughts. I found it. It is a speech I gave at Oxford University during the summer of 2001 to a marvelous group of students who had studied with me during August. I have reproduced the entire presentation in order to indicate the political and social values, which have guided me in more than 30 years of university teaching and public service. Although presented in a different context this speech illustrates what the War on Terrorism is all about for me. I would encourage all of my students to go through the same exercise—this War will be long and it will involve great sacrifice from all of us. It would be best if we have our moral compasses set before the arduous journey begins

Oxford, England, Aug. 3, 2001

I have been a Professor for a very long time—longer than most of you have been alive. I have worked for three American Presidents, served on American ships of war, served in the intelligence community, taught in several universities, been the target of a terrorist attack, written several peculiarly unpopular books, and been a part of several presidential campaigns and inaugurations. In all of this, I want you to know that I have never done anything I have been more proud of and more pleased with than our month together in England—our month together in the world's first and still greatest university—Oxford University.

Wherever we all journey I shall always have a wonderful, enduring, inspiring memory of this extraordinary time in my life. It would be beneath the moment to thank you so I shall just say God speed and God bless all of you—which I bet He will.

I feel compelled to share two last thoughts. Of all the ideas in all the history of the world, the most compelling and the most contagious is the idea of freedom. The strange, almost bizarre notion that men and women shall be allowed to control their own destinies in their own way. Nothing, absolutely nothing men have ever thought about or conceived compares to this simple, overwhelming idea. I should like you to know that freedom as you and I know it—freedom in its real sense—freedom that makes life wonderful and exhilarating comes from this island and was promoted universally by these wonderful island people. Lady Thatcher once said that England's greatest contribution to the world was the creation of its colonies in America, which ultimately led to the creation of America itself—a special land created solely for the purpose of advancing human freedom. Freedom is our creed, it is our ideology, it is our life, it is our mission, and it is our destiny.

Together the English-speaking world has taught, yes taught the world about democracy and law. We have and continue to provide the New Jerusalem and the New City on the Hill from which the oppressed and the downtrodden are inspired.

I would ask only that you understand this heritage and understand the pride you should attach to it. All cultures and all civilizations are interesting. All are unique. All dazzle the imagination but none has even remotely advanced the cause of humanity and civilization, as has England. Come back, come back to England—be inspired and remember Lord Nelson—"England expects every man shall do his duty." I expect that all of you shall do your duty.

Help the world to be free, help a little child, help someone who is forlorn, help someone who is lonely, help someone who reaches out to you, help someone to be free and in the process help yourself by being more than just yourself. Dream with me the ultimate, impossible dream—we can end war, we can end slavery, we can end oppression and terrorism. Try to remember the most important question of your lives is not "why"—it is "why not."

I wish you well, I wish you luck, I shall think of you always. Try, please try desperately to remember that the greatest engine for progress and freedom is the Academy. The Academy with all its idiosyncrasies and all of its problems is still an ivory tower of civility, decency, fair play, and good cheer. Decide now that you are an academic and will be an academic to the end of your life. Recall what we have accomplished and what we can do—never leave us and you shall always be one of God's special children. Promise you will tell all who will listen what this special, friendly, gentle placed called Oxford really means—it is the final shining City on the Hill—a city you shall be part of forever.

Finally I would like to add an email message I sent to one thousand students a few days after the attacks on New York and Washington, D.C.

San Diego, California, Sept. 21, 2001

    Although most of you know my views about the President, I thought I might add that I believe last night's speech to the nation was the most remarkable moment in the history of the modern presidency. It was not just the most important speech in George Bush's life—it was the most important speech in the life of the modern presidency itself.

    I am amazed, thrilled, and of course pleased that the President is able to adjust to the enormous task before him with such remarkable ease. I remember last year when I shook hands with the President being nearly overwhelmed by his confidence, good cheer, and charm. I remember feeling without any qualification that he was a man who would ultimately be an heroic President. I had no idea it would come in this form but the warrior-statesman is at hand. He is clearly comfortable with his destiny—which is to lead the world's greatest nation through one of its darkest and most complicated periods. I feel absolutely confident that he knows exactly what to do and will do it. All of this is going to be more difficult than you now realize but in the end we will not falter and we will not fail. Leadership is the key ingredient to success and on that front America is ready. The Armed Forces will strike and it will be frightening and it will at first accomplish very little. Then they will strike again and then the nation through every resource at its disposal will strike and that will bring victory.

    I have been invited to speak to the cadets at Sandhurst, Great Britain's West Point. I intend to tell them what I want you to always remember—America was not put on this earth to be destroyed by a band of psychopathic murderers. We shall lead the world to a new Golden Age and we shall look back on these days as part of our proudest moment. You are lucky to be part of it—before victory comes you will be able to help in a million ways, and sometime off in the future you will be able to tell your children and your grandchildren that when freedom and civilization called, you were there.

Be brave, be confidant, and God speed:
Dr. Mike Stoddard

PART V
Country Profiles

Afghanistan

Background:

Afghanistan was invaded and occupied by the Soviet Union in 1979. The USSR was forced to withdraw 10 years later by anti-communist Mujahidin forces supplied and trained by the US, Saudi Arabia, and Pakistan. Fighting subsequently continued among the various Mujahidin factions, but the fundamentalist Islamic Taliban movement was able to seize most of the country. The Taliban was destroyed by the US Coalition by the end of 2001. The country suffers from enormous poverty, a crumbling infrastructure, and widespread land mines

Geography:

Continent: Asia
Total Area: 647,500 sq km, landlocked, slightly smaller than Texas
Terrain: Mostly rugged mountains, plains in north and Southwest

Climate:

Arid to semi-arid, cold winters and hot summers

Environmental Issues:

> Soil degradation; overgrazing; deforestation (most of the remaining forests are being cut down for fuel and building materials); desertification

Population:

> 29,928,987 (42 % under 15 years of age)

Ethnic Groups:

> Pashtun 44%, Tajik 25%, Hazara 10%, Minor Ethnic Groups: Aimaks, Turkmen, Baloch, and others 13%, Uzbek 8%

Infant Mortality Rate:

> 142.48 deaths/1,000 live births

Average Life Expectancy:

> 46.24 years

Religions:

> Sunni Muslim 80%, Shi'a Muslim 19%, other 1%

Language:

> Pashtu 35%, Afghan Persian (Dari) 50%, Turkic languages (primarily Uzbek and Turkmen) 11%, 30 minor languages (primarily Balochi and Pashai) 4%, much bilingualism

Literacy: *(definition: age 15 and over can read and write)*

> Total: 36%, male: 51%, female: 21%

Government:

> Islamic Republic

Capital:

> Kabul

Constitution:

> Constitutional democracy established June 16, 2004

Economy:

> Afghanistan is an extremely poor, landlocked country, highly dependent on farming and livestock raising (sheep and goats). The economy has been all but destroyed by the political and military upheavals during two decades of war, including the nearly 10-year Soviet military occupation (which ended 02/15/89). During that conflict one-third of the population fled the country, with Pakistan and Iran sheltering a combined peak of more than six million refugees. In early 2000, two million Afghan refugees remained in Pakistan and about 1.4 million in Iran. Gross domestic product has fallen substantially over the past 20 years because of the loss of labor and capital and the disruption of trade and transport; severe drought added to the nation's difficulties in 1998-2000. The majority of the population continues to suffer from insufficient food, clothing, housing, and medical care. Afghanistan was by far the largest producer of opium poppies in 2000, and narcotics trafficking is a major source of revenue

GDP: *(per capita)*

> $800

Economic Aid

$8.9 billion in development aid promised by the US Coalition for 2004 - 2009

Currency:

Afghani (AFA)

Televisions:

100,000

Transnational Issues:

Illicit Drugs: World's largest illicit opium producer, surpassing Burma (potential production in 1999 – 1,670 metric tons; cultivation in 1999 – 51,500 hectares, a 23% increase over 1998); a major source of hashish; increasing number of heroin-processing laboratories being set up in the country; major political factions in the country profit from drug trade

Afghanistan Timeline

1946 - Shah Mahmud became PM; Afghanistan admitted to the UN
1949 - First free elections held
1951 - United States halted economic aid
1956 - Arms pacts signed with USSR and Czechoslovakia
1959 - Aid pact signed with USSR; President Eisenhower visited Kabul
1961 - Diplomatic relations cut with Pakistan
1963 - King dismissed PM Daoud; Mohammud Yusuf appointed PM; Diplomatic relations reestablished with Pakistan
1964 - New constitution promulgated
1965 - Mohammad Hashim Maiwandwal became PM; all adults were enfranchised
1973 - King Zahir abdicated
1978 - Daoud overthrown in coup; Taraki became President; Friendship Treaty signed with USSR
1979 - Soviet Union commited 30,000 troops to Afghanistan; US Ambassador Adolph Dubs shot and killed in Kabul; President Taraki killed in a coup; Hafizullah Amis named President and killed in coup; Babrak Karmal, pro-Moscow hardliner, installed as President

1980 - Approximately 800,000 Afghans crossed border into Pakistan; Afghanistan suspended from the Conference of Islamic States
1986 - Mujahidin demanded unconditional Soviet withdrawal
1988 - Soviet troop withdrawal began; direct talks between Mujahidin and Soviets; talks brokedown
1989 - State of emergency declared
1992 - Najibullah overthrown; elections held; Rabbani declared President
1993 - Peace talks brokered by Pakistan; compromise met; Hekmatyar became Prime Minister
1994 - Rise of the Taliban as fighting force; opposed "un-Islamic" activities of government and factional leaders
1996 - Taliban Militia seized Kabul; opposition coalition formed as United Islamic Front for the Salvation of Afghanistan (UIFSA)
1997 - Taliban seized then lost Mazar-e-Sharif, NIM stronghold in northern Afghanistan; incured heavy losses; infighting rampant in UIFSA; external powers continued proxy war
1998 - Taliban captured Mazar-e-Sharif; UIFSA collapsed; Taliban controlled 90% of country; continued pressure on remaining opposition; Taliban sought UN seat and international recognition
2001 - Taliban sponsored terrorist attacks on the World Trade Center and Pentagon on September 11; Taliban evacuated Kabul under coalition attacks on November 13
2002 - The US military campaign was completed; the government of Hamid Kaizar was established; elections were promised; UN peacekeepers were stationed throughout the nation led by 5,000 British and Turkish Special Forces
2003 - The Kaizar government made progress in stabilizing the economy; an Afghan national army was created; the central government maintained control of Kabul with only limited influence over the rest of Afghanistan
2004 - Draft Constitution calling for a powerful executive and a two-house assembly, a 9 member supreme court, and a central bank; Presidential elections held in October 2004; Hamid Kaizar elected the first President of a free Iraq; US forces continued to pursue Al Qaeda in the south along the Pakistani-Afghan border
2005 – Afghan security forces in control of most of the nation; radical reduction of jihadist attacks
2006 – Native forces increased; US deployment reduced
2007- NATO involvement increased

Bahrain

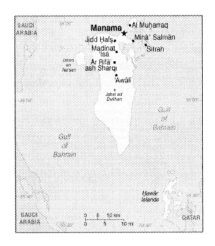

Background:

Bahrain's small size and central location among Persian Gulf countries requires it to play a delicate balancing act in foreign affairs among its larger neighbors. Possessing minimal oil reserves, Bahrain has turned to petroleum processing and refining, and has transformed itself into an international banking center. The new Amir is pushing economic and political reforms, and has worked to improve relations with the Shi'a community. In 2001, the International Court of Justice awarded the Hawar Islands, long disputed with Qatar, to Bahrain. Bahrain allows the US Navy substantial basing rights. Tiny Bahrain has been a faithful US ally and remains essential to US policy in the area. Bahrain's problems are compounded by its large Shi'a population

Geography:

Total area: 620 sq. km, 3.5 times the size of Washington, D.C.
Terrain: Mostly low desert plain rising gently to low central escarpment

Climate:

    Arid, mild, pleasant winters; very hot, humid summers

Environmental Issues:

    Desertification resulting from the degradation of limited arable land, periods of drought, and dust storms; coastal degradation (damage to coastlines, coral reefs, and sea vegetation) resulting from oil spills and other discharges from large tankers, oil refineries, and distribution stations; no natural fresh water resources so that groundwater and sea water are the only sources for all water needs

Population:

    688,345 (29% under 15 years of age)

Ethnic Groups:

    Bahraini 63%, Asian 19%, other Arab 10%, Iranian 8%

Infant Mortality Rate:

    19.77 deaths/1,000 live births

Average Life Expectancy:

    73.72 years

Religions:

    Shi'a Muslim 70%, Sunni Muslim 30%

Language:

    Arabic, English, Farsi, Urdu

Literacy: *(definition: age 15 and older can read and write)*

    Total population: 89.1%
    Male: 91.9%
    Female: 85%

Government:

    Constitutional Monarchy

Capital:

    Manama

Economy:

    In Bahrain, petroleum production and refining account for about 60% of export receipts 60% of government revenues, and 30% of GDP. With its highly developed communication and transport facilities, Bahrain is home to numerous multinational firms with business in the Gulf. Bahrain is dependent on Saudi Arabia for oil revenue granted as aid. A large share of exports consists of petroleum products made from imported crude

GDP: *(per capita)*

    $19,000

Economic Aid:

    $150 million since 1992 from Saudi Arabia, The UAE and Kuwait

Currency:

    Bahraini Dinar (BHD)

Televisions:

    275,000

Military:

> Home of the US Gulf Fleet; Bahrain depends on US military protection for its survival

Bahrain Timeline

1892 - Ruler of Bahrain signed treaty of protection with UK
1902 - British political agent assigned to Bahrain
1913 - Anglo-Turkish convention ensured Bahrain's existence as a sovereign state
1923 - Establishment of formal government structure and bureaucracy
1930 - Bahrain Petroleum Company (BAPCO) created
1932 - Discovery of oil; production started in 1934
1935 - BAPCO refinery built; first in the Persian Gulf
1939 - UK awarded disputed Hawar Islands to Bahrain
1958 - Offshore boundary with Saudi Arabia delimited by treaty
1968 - UK announced intention to terminate treaty obligations with Bahrain and other Persian Gulf sheikdoms by end of 1971
1970 - Iran relinquished longstanding claim to Bahrain
1971 - Bahrain, Qatar, and seven Trucial states announced provisional formation of the Federation of the Arab Emirates; Bahrain chose separation and secured independence from British protection and suzerainty; 'Isa becomes first Amir
1970 -72 - Oil production peaked
1973 - Amir enacted new constitution
1981 - Gulf Cooperation Council (GCC) founded
1986 - Confrontation with Qatar over disputed offshore reef; causeway linking Bahrain with Saudi Arabia opened
1990 - Bahrain joined coalition forces to oust Iraq from Kuwait
2001 - Bahrain announced support for the US Coalition and continued use of bases for US Military Forces in its Afghan campaign
2002 - Riots broke out in Manama protesting US support for Israel and the Israeli incursion into the West Bank
2003 - Bahrain provided unqualified support for the US Coalition in its Iraqi campaign
2004 - Bahrain offered $1 billion in loans to the Iraq Reconstruction Fund
2005 – Local elections held; women allowed to vote
2007 – Bahrain continued to support US foreign policy objectives

Egypt

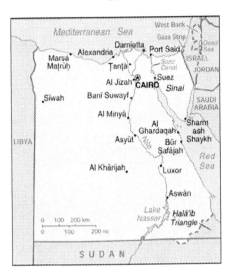

Background:

Nominally independent from the UK in 1922, Egypt acquired full sovereignty following World War II. The completion of the Aswan High Dam in 1971 and the resultant Lake Nasser have altered the time-honored place of the Nile River in the agriculture and ecology of Egypt. A rapidly growing population (the largest in the Arab world), limited arable land, and dependence on the Nile all continue to overtax resources and stress society. President Mubarak has consistently played the role of mediator between Arab radicals and conservatives. Egypt's support for US efforts in the region has been critical. Egypt's dilemma illustrates the problem of many Middle Eastern nations as the regime constantly wrestles with the terrorist group, the Egyptian Jihad, within its borders

Geography:

Continent: Africa

Total Area: 1,001,450 sq km, slightly more than three times the size of New Mexico

Terrain: Vast desert plateau interrupted by Nile valley and delta

Climate:

Desert; hot, dry summers with moderate winters

Environmental Issues:

Agricultural land being lost to urbanization and windblown sands; increasing soil salination below Aswan Dam; desertification; oil pollution threatening coral reefs, beaches, and marine habitats; other water pollution from agricultural pesticides, raw sewage, and industrial effluents; very limited natural fresh water resources away from the Nile which is the only perennial water source; rapid growth in population overstraining natural resources

Population:

77,505,756 (34% under 15 years of age)

Ethnic Groups:

Eastern Hamitic stock (Egyptians, Bedouins, and Berbers) 99%, Greek, Nubian, Armenian, other European (primarily Italian and French) 1%

Infant Mortality Rate:

35.26 deaths/1,000 live births

Average Life Expectancy:

70.41 years

Religions:

Muslim (mostly Sunni) 94%, Coptic Christian and other 6%

Language:

Arabic (official), English and French widely understood by educated classes

Literacy: *(definition: age 15 and older can read and write)*

Total population: 57.7%
Male: 68.3%
Female: 46.9%

Government:

Republic/Presidential dictatorship

Capital:

Cairo

Economy:

A series of IMF arrangements – along with massive external debt relief resulting from Egypt's participation in the Gulf war coalition – helped Egypt improve its macroeconomic performance during the 1990s. Sound fiscal and monetary policies through the mid-1990s helped to tame inflation, slash budget deficits, and build up foreign reserves, while structural reforms such a privatization and new business legislation prompted increased foreign investment

GDP: (per capita)

$4,200

Economic Aid:

Recipient: $2.8 billion; mostly from the US

Currency:

> Egyptian pound (EGP)

Televisions:

> 7.7 million

Transnational Issues:

> A transit point for Southwest Asian and Southeast Asian heroin and opium moving to Europe, Africa, and the US, popular stop for Nigerian couriers

Egypt Timeline

1882 - British occupation of Egypt and virtual inclusion within British Empire began
1914 - Egypt became a British protectorate
1922 - Egyptian independence declared by UK
1936 - Anglo-Egyptian treaty of mutual defense and alliance signed; occupation of Egypt terminated
1945 - Arab League founded in Cairo with seven charter members
1948-49 - Arab League troops, including Egyptians attacked new state of Israel; armistice agreement signed in 1949; Gaza Strip placed under Egyptian administration
1952 - "Arab Officers," led by Lt. Col. Abdul Nasser, overthrew King Faruk; Egypt declared a republic in 1953
1956 - Nasser nationalized Suez Canal Company; Suez War; Israel launched attack Into Sinai; French and British forces invaded Suez Canal Zone
1958-61 - Union of Egypt and Syria into United Arab Republic; after Syrian secession, Egypt retained name of UAR until 1971
1960 - Soviet aided construction of Aswan High Dam began; completed by 1970
1962 - Egyptian troops dispatched to Yemen to assist republican forces; confrontation with Saudi Arabia ensued
1967 - Nasser closed the Strait of Tiran to Israeli shipping; June War brought Israeli occupation of Gaza Strip and Sinai Peninsula; Suez Canal closed

- 1969 - "War of Attrition" against Israel
- 1970 - President Nasser died of heart attack; Anwar Sadat became president
- 1972 - Sadat ordered withdrawal of Soviet military advisors
- 1973 - October war, Egypt and Syria launched surprise attack against Israel
- 1974 - Disengagement of Israeli forces from Sinai began
- 1977 - Sadat visited Jerusalem
- 1979 - Treaty of Peace between Egypt and Israel signed in Washington, DC; Arab League rescinded Cairo's membership
- 1981 - Religious extremists assassinated Sadat; Mubarak approved as successor
- 1982 - Sinai Peninsula restored to Egypt after nearly 15 years of Israeli occupation
- 1989 - Taba area returned to Egypt ending the last territorial dispute with Israel; Cairo's membership in Arab League restored
- 1990-91 - Egypt contributed troops and political support to Gulf War effort
- 1993 - Islamic extremists began campaign of violence against Egypt's tourist industry and senior Egyptian leadership
- 1995 - President Mubarak escaped attempted assassination planned by Osama bin Laden while on state visit in Sudan
- 1997 - Islamic insurgents killed 58 tourists at historic site in Luxor
- 2001 - President Mubarak supported the US Coalition in Afghanistan but urged US assistance in the resolution of the Israeli/Palestinian conflict
- 2002 - Egypt led the Arab coalition demanding Israeli restraint in the West Bank and Gaza
- 2003 - President Mubarak offered limited support for the US invasion of Iraq; Mubarak announced: "The War was brought about by the policies of Saddam Hussein"
- 2004 - Offered technical assistance for Iraq at the Iraq Donor Conference
- 2005 – Increasing democratic resistance to government control; Mubarak "reelected" in a tightly controlled election
- 2007 – Increased internal efforts to wipe out terrorists

Iran

Background:

Known as Persia until 1935, Iran became an Islamic republic in 1979 after the ruling shah was forced into exile. Conservative clerical forces subsequently crushed Westernizing liberal elements. Militant Iranian students seized the US Embassy in Tehran on November 4, 1979 and held it until January 20, 1981. During 1980-88, Iran fought a bloody, indecisive war with Iraq over disputed territory. Iran has sponsored terrorism for several years. Iran's new, more moderate President may provide an opening for a change in Iranian policy

Geography:

Total area: 1.648 million sq km, slightly larger than Alaska
Terrain: Rugged, mountainous rim; high, central basin with deserts, mountains; small, discontinuous plains along both coasts

Climate:

Mostly arid or semiarid, subtropical along Caspian coast

Environmental Issues:

> Air Pollution, especially in urban areas, from vehicle emissions, refinery operations, and industrial effluents; deforestation; overgrazing; desertification; oil pollution in the Persian Gulf; inadequate supplies of potable water

Population:

> 68,017,860 (29% under 15 years of age)

Ethnic Groups:

> Persian 51%, Azeri 24%, Gilaki and Mazandarani 8%, Kurd 7%, Arab 3%, Lur 2%, Baloch 2%, Turkmen 2%, other 1%

Infant Mortality Rate:

> 44.17 deaths/1,000 live births

Average Life Expectancy:

> 69.35 years

Religions:

> Shi'a Muslim 89%, Sunni Muslim 10%, Zoroastrian, Jewish, Christian, and Baha'l 1%

Language:

> Persian and Persian dialects 58%, Turkic and Turkic dialects 26%, Kurdish 9%, Luri 2%, Balochi 1%, Arabic 1%, Turkish 1%, other 2%

Literacy: *(definition: age 15 and older can read and write)*

> Total population: 79.4%
> Male: 85.6%
> Female: 73%

Government:

> Theocratic Republic; four elections held from 1997-2001 with a limited impact on the ruling religious elites

Capital:

> Tehran

Economy:

> Iran's economy is a mixture of central planning, state ownership of oil and other large enterprises, village agriculture, and small-scale private trading and service ventures. President Khatami has continued to follow the market reform plans of former President Rafsanjani and has indicated that he will diversify Iran's oil-reliant economy although he has made little progress toward that goal

GDP: *(per capita)*

> $7,700

Economic Aid

> $408 million

Currency:

> Iranian rial (IRR)

Televisions:

> 4.61 million

Transnational Issues:

> Despite substantial interdiction efforts, Iran remains a key transshipment point for Southwest Asian heroin to Europe; domestic consumption of narcotics remains a persistent problem and Iranian

press reports estimate that there are at least 1.2 million drug users in the country

Iran Timeline

1906 - Fundamental Laws (National Constitution) adopted by Iranian Parliament under Qajar dynasty monarch
1908 - Discovery of oil in Khuzistan; commercial production began by 1912
1921 - Successful coup led by Reza Khan
1925 - Reza Khan crowned and ruled as Reza Shah Pahlavi for nearly 16 years
1941 - UK and Soviet Union invaded Iran to counter threat of expanding German influence...Reza Shah abdicated in favor of son Mohammad Reza Shah
1953 - Mosadek ousted by coup; Shah assumed power
1961 - Widespread political, economic, and social reforms; the Shah's White Revolution
1963-65 - Ayatollah Khomeini, religious leader in Qom, arrested for speaking out against the Shah; exiled to Turkey; fled to Iraq
1967 - Coronation of Mohammad Reza Shah
1970 - Shah gave up Iran's longstanding claims to Bahrain
1978 - Domestic turmoil swept the country in opposition to Shah's rule
1979 - Shah departed; Khomeini returned after 15 year exile; Islamic Republic proclaimed; US Embassy occupied and diplomats taken hostage
1980 - US rescue attempt of hostages failed in Iranian desert; outbreak of war with Iraq
1981 - Release of American hostages from US Embassy in Tehran
1986-87 - Increased Iranian and Iraqi attacks on ships in the Persian Gulf; the "tanker war"
1988 - Cease-fire ended eight-year war with Iraq
1989 - Death of Ayatollah Khomeini; succeeded by Ayatollah Ali Hoseini Khamenei; Rafsanjani elected President
1991 - Iran maintained effective neutrality during Gulf War; played host to over one million refugees from Iraq
1997 - Mohammad Khatami, a political moderate, elected President in a landslide
2001 - Iran first condemned the US attacks on Afghanistan; changed to limited support; condemned terrorism; President Bush indicated US interest in an opening to Iran

2002 - Iran identified by President Bush as part of the "axis of evil;" condemned by the US for continued support of terrorism particularly in Palestine; condemned by the US for the continued development of nuclear weapons; Iran threatened to destroy all of the oil of the Persian Gulf if attacked by the US

2003 - Iran condemned but stayed out of the US war in Iraq

2004 - Allowed Iraq to export oil through Iranian ports and supply its neighbors with electricity and gas; the International Atomic Energy Agency (IAEA) investigated Iran's "suspicious" nuclear activities; the governors of the IAEA imposed a firm deadline for Iran to clarify past actions, allow unfettered future inspections, and suspend work related to producing bomb-quality materials; Iran announced it would not share its intelligence on suspected Al-Qaeda members with the US; Iran accepted the EU – 3 proposal for the development of peaceful nuclear energy

2005 – Collapse of the EU – US attempts to stop Iranian development of nuclear facilities; The ascension to power of a Jihadist President who called for the elimination of Israel

2006 – US Iranian talks regarding Iran's nuclear program; President Bush continued to insist "diplomacy will work" but refused to take the military action "off the table"

2007- US-EU efforts to coordinate a UN embargo of Iran until its nuclear program is stopped; no realistic progress in stopping Iran from acquiring nuclear weapons; continued references by Pres. Bush that diplomacy will work but if it does not all American options are open

Iraq

Background:

Formerly part of the Ottoman Empire, Iraq became an independent kingdom in 1932. A "republic" was proclaimed in 1958, but in actuality a series of military strongmen have ruled the country since then, the latest being Saddam Hussein. Territorial disputes with Iran led to an inconclusive and costly eight-year war (1980-1988). In August 1990 Iraq seized Kuwait, but was expelled by US-led, UN coalition forces during January-February 1991. The victors did not occupy Iraq, however, thus allowing the regime to stay in control. Following Kuwait's liberation, the UN Security Council required Iraq to scrap all weapons of mass destruction and long range missiles and to allow UN verification inspections. UN trade sanctions remained in effect due to incomplete Iraqi compliance with relevant UNSC resolutions. All UN inspectors were thrown out of the country in 1998. Iraq continued to develop weapons of mass destruction including weapons which could be used in bioterrorism. President Bush said: "We are watching Saddam very carefully." The President consistently referred to Saddam as evil. The US led Coalition invaded Iraq in March 2003. A US sponsored interim government was established in May. The Coalition maintained order as an occupying force.

Geography:

Continent: Asia
Total Area: 437,072 sq km, slightly more than twice the size of Idaho
Terrain: Mostly broad plains; reedy marshes along Iranian border in south with large flooded areas; mountains along borders with Iran and Turkey

Climate:

Mostly desert; mild to cool winters with dry, hot, cloudless summers; northern mountainous regions along Iranian and Turkish borders experience cold winters with occasionally heavy snows that melt in early spring, sometimes causing extensive flooding in central and southern Iraq

Environmental Issues:

Government water control projects have drained most of the inhabited marsh areas east of An Nasiryah by drying up or diverting the feeder streams and rivers; a once sizable population of Shi'a Muslims, who have inhabited these areas for thousands of years, has been displaced; furthermore, the destruction of the natural habitat poses serious threats to the area's wildlife populations; inadequate supplies of potable water; development of Tigris-Euphrates Rivers system contingent upon agreements with Turkey; air and water pollution; soil degradation (salination) and erosion; desertification

Population:

26,074,906 (41% under 15 years of age)

Ethnic Groups:

Arab 75-80%, Kurdish 15-20%, Turkoman, Assyrian or other 5%

Infant Mortality Rate:

    55.16 deaths/1,000 live births

Average Life Expectancy:

    67.81 years

Religions:

    Muslim 97% (Shi'a 60-65%, Sunni 32-37%), Christian or other 3%

Language:

    Arabic, Kurdish (official in Kurdish regions), Assyrian, Armenian

Literacy: *(definition: age 15 and older can read and write)*

    Total population: 40.4%
    Male: 55.9%
    Female: 24.4%

Government:

    Constitutional Republic established Jan 30, 2005

Capital:

    Baghdad

Economy:

    Iraq's economy is dominated by the oil sector, which has traditionally provided about 95% of foreign exchange earnings. In the 1980s, financial problems caused by massive expenditures in the eight-year war with Iran and damage to oil export facilities by Iran led the government to implement austerity measures, borrow heavily, and later reschedule foreign debt payments; Iraq suffered economic losses of at least $100 billion from the war. After the end of hostilities in 1988, oil exports gradually increased with the construction of new pipelines and restoration of damaged facilities. Iraq's seizure of Kuwait in August 1990, subsequent international economic sanctions, and damage from military action by an international coalition beginning in January 1991 drastically reduced economic activity. Although government policies supporting large military and internal security forces and allocating resources to key supporters of the regime hurt the economy, implementation of the UN's oil-for-food program in December 1996 helped improve conditions for the average Iraqi citizen. For the first six month phase of the program, Iraq was allowed to export limited amounts of oil in exchange for food, medicine, and some infrastructure spare parts. In December 1999, the UN Security Council authorized Iraq to export under the program as much oil as required to meet humanitarian needs. The elimination of the Hussein regime in 2003 brought about the total disruption of the economy.

GDP: *(per capita)*

$3,500

Economic Aid

Recipient: $33 billion for 2004 - 2007

Currency:

New Iraqi dinar (IQD) introduced by the US in 2003

Televisions:

1.75 million

Transnational Issues:

Iran and Iraq restored diplomatic relations in 1990 but are still trying to work out written agreements, settling outstanding disputes from their eight-year war concerning border demarcation, prisoners-of-war, and freedom of navigation and sovereignty over the Shatt al Arab waterway; in November 1994, Iraq formally accepted the UN-Resolutions 687 (1991), 773 (1993), and 883 (1993); this formally ended earlier claims to Kuwait and to Bublyan and Warbaj islands although the government continued periodic rhetorical challenges; dispute over water development plans by Turkey for the Tigris and Euphrates rivers

Iraq Timeline

1534-1918 - Area ruled by Ottoman Turks
1912 - Turkish Petroleum Co. formed; concession given to British by 1914
1913 - Boundary with Kuwait defined by Anglo-Turkish convention
1920 - Mandate for Iraq awarded to UK by League of Nations
1921 - Hashemite monarchy established under King Faysal
1922 - Boundary with Saudi Arabia agreed
1927 - Discovery of oil north of Karkuk
1932 - Iraq achieved independence
1936 – First military coup d'etat
1948-49 - Iraqi troops joined in Arab League invasion of Israel
1958 - Hashemite Kingdoms, Iraq and Jordan joined Arab Union Federation; King Faysal assassinated in coup; General Quasim took power
1961 - Quasim claimed Kuwait as integral part of Iraq; Kurds began armed revolt against Baghdad
1963 - Quasim killed in military coup; Iraq renounced claim on Kuwait
1966 - Cease fire between Kurds and government forces
1967 - June war with Israel; Iraqi airfields attacked
1968 - Arab Socialist Ba'th (Resurrection) Party seized power
1970 - Announced settlement ended Kurdish rebellion in the north
1972 - Iraq Petroleum Co., a consortium of Western companies, was nationalized
1979 - Saddam Hussein emerged as President and Chairman of RCC
1980 - Unilateral denunciation of Baghdad Treaty; war with Iran started
1982 - Export pipeline via Syria closed
1984 - Diplomatic relations restored with US
1988 - Cease fire ended eight-year war with Iran; Iraq reasserted claim to Kuwait
1990 - Invasion of Kuwait; world community imposed economic embargo
1991 - Iraq forcibly ejected from Kuwait by coalition forces; suffered significant infrastructure damage
1991-98 - Iraq placed under UN sanctions severely degrading their economy

2001 - Saddam Hussein announced continued support for the Taliban; denied any involvement with the New York or the Anthrax attacks

2002 - Iraq identified by President Bush as part of the "axis of evil;" condemned for the continued support of terrorism; condemned for the continued development of nuclear weapons; ordered to readmit UN inspectors

2003 - US military attack; elimination of the regime of Saddam Hussein; establishment of three military zones – British, Polish, and American; creation of an interim government

2004 - $87 billion committed by the US for Iraqi security and reconstruction; $36 billion pledged over 5 years by other Coalition members; 150,000 personnel recruited for the new Iraqi security forces; massive reconstruction started of hospitals, banks, masques, oil refineries, hydroelectric systems, communication systems, schools, and universities; 90 percent of the nation was stable; disruptions continued in the Sunni Triangle; Iraqi Governing Council announced the creation of the constitutional commission; sovereignty was returned to Iraq on June 30; elections scheduled for the 275-member National Assembly are for January 30; Japan, the US, Russia and most European countries agreed to write off 80% of Iraq's $40 billion debt

2005 – Election of a 275 member national parliament; 60 percent turnout in Iraq's first national election; ratification of a democratic constitution in October; Shi'a Ibrahim al-Jafaari selected Prime Minister; a Kurdish President, Jalal Talabani, assumed power; Sunni Hajim al-Hassani selected as Speaker of the new Parliament; election of a new Government on December 15th

2006 – Sovereign Iraqi government established; US forces cut to 100,000; Iraqi forces increased to 300,000; surprise visit to Baghdad by President Bush; US forces killed al-Zargawi and captured considerable intelligence documents

2007- Major increase in sectarian violence; little progress in the central governments ability to maintain order in the Sunni Triangle

Israel

Background:

Following World War II, the British withdrew from their mandate of Palestine, and the UN partitioned the area into Arab and Jewish states, an arrangement rejected by the Arabs. Subsequently, the Israelis defeated the Arabs in a series of wars without ending the deep tensions between the two sides. On April 25, 1982, Israel withdrew from the Sinai pursuant to the 1979 Israel-Egypt Peace Treaty. Outstanding territorial and other disputes with Jordan were resolved in the October 26, 1994 Israel-Jordan treaty of Peace. On May 25, 2000, Israel withdrew unilaterally from southern Lebanon, which it had occupied since 1982. Israel is a staunch supporter of the

US position on terrorism. Israel's greatest fear is that somehow the War on Terrorism might weaken America's commitment to the Jewish State. Israel "quietly" supported the US attacks on Afghanistan (2001) and Iraq (2003)

Geography:

Total Area: 20,770 sq. km, slightly smaller than New Jersey
Terrain: Negev desert in the south; low coastal plain; central mountains; Jordan Rift Valley

Climate:

Temperate; hot and dry in southern and eastern desert areas

Environmental Issues:

Limited arable land and natural fresh water resources pose serious constraints; desertification; air pollution from industrial and vehicle emissions; groundwater pollution from industrial and domestic waste, chemical fertilizers, and pesticides party to: biodiversity, climate change, desertification, endangered species, hazardous wastes, nuclear test ban, ozone layer protection, ship pollution, wetlands

Population:

6,276,883 (27% under 15 years of age)

Ethnic Groups:

Jewish 80.1% (Europe/America-born 32.1%, Israel-born 20.8%, Africa-born 14.6%, Asia-born 12.6%), non-Jewish 19.9% (mostly Arab)

Infant Mortality Rate:

7.37 deaths/1,000 live births

Average Life Expectancy:

> 79.02 years

Religions:

> Jewish 80.1%, Muslim 14.6% (mostly Sunni Muslim), Christian 2.1%, other 3.2%

Language:

> Hebrew (official), Arabic used officially for Arab minority, English most commonly used foreign language

Literacy: *(definition: age 15 and older can read and write)*

> Total population: 95%
> Male: 97%
> Female: 93%

Government:

> Parliamentary Democracy

Capital:

> Jerusalem

Economy:

> Israel has a technologically advanced market economy with substantial government participation. It depends on imports of crude oil, grains, raw materials, and military equipment. Despite limited natural resources, Israel has intensively developed its agricultural and industrial sectors over the past 20 years. Israel is largely self-sufficient in food production except for grains. Cut diamonds, high-technology equipment, and agricultural products (fruits and vegetables) are the leading exports. Israel usually posts sizeable

deficits, which are covered by the US, which is its major source of economic and military aid. The influx of Jewish immigrants from the former USSR topped 750,000 during the period 1989-99, bringing the population of Israel from the former Soviet Union to 1 million, one-sixth of the total population

GDP: *(per capita)*

$20,800

Economic Aid:

$3 billion from the US

Currency:

New Israeli Shekel (ILS)

Televisions:

1.69 million

Transnational Issues:

Increasingly concerned about cocaine and heroin abuse; drugs arrive from Lebanon and increasingly Jordan

Israel Timeline

1948 - Creation of the Jewish State
1956 - The Suez War
1967 - The Six Day War—Israeli acquisition of Gaza, Sinai, the West Bank, the Golan Heights, and all of Jerusalem
1973 - The Yom Kippur War—US shuttle diplomacy
1982 - Israel invaded Lebanon in an attempt to destroy the Palestine Liberation Organization (PLO) bases along Israel's northern border
1987 - The Intifadah, a period of protest in the West Bank and Gaza started
1989 - Soviet Union began to collapse; Russian Jews began new wave of immigration into Israel

- 1991 - During the Gulf War, Iraq targeted Haifa and Tel Aviv for Scud missile attacks; about 14,500 people, nearly the entire Jewish population of Ethiopia, were airlifted to Israel
- 1993 - Israel and the PLO agreed on a framework for autonomy in the West Bank and Gaza Strip; a final peace treaty was foreseen by 1999
- 1994 - Israeli troops pulled out of Gaza and Jericho, handing over control to Palestinian police; other West Bank towns followed; Jordan and Israel signed a peace treaty; a Palestinian suicide bomber killed 22 on a Tel Aviv bus
- 1995 - Prime Minister Yitzhak Rabin assassinated
- 1996 - Islamic suicide bombers killed 63 in Jerusalem and Tel Aviv
- 1997 - Benjamin Netanyahu's cabinet reaffirmed its decision to build a Jewish neighborhood in East Jerusalem, despite warnings of Palestinian violence; suicide bombings increased, with deadly incidents in Tel Aviv and Jerusalem; Palestinian authority legalized the death sentence for Arabs who sold land to Jews
- 2001 - Prime Minister Barak resigned; replaced by Prime Minister Sharon; Israel reoccupied Palestinian areas; Secretary of State Powell announced a new US initiative to resume the peace process
- 2002 - Israel announced the end to all further contact with Arafat; collapse of the peace process; hardening positions on both sides of Palestinian-Israeli conflict; April invasion of the West Bank and Gaza in reaction to the suicide bombers; Arafat isolated to his headquarters in Ramallah; May withdrawal from most of the Territories; Arafat's confinement ended with President Bush's personal intervention; the US called for reform within the PLO implying Arafat would have to be replaced by democratic leadership; President Bush proclaimed that forcing the Israelis to trade land for peace meant that peace would have to be guaranteed; Sharon reelected
- 2003 - The US announced its "roadmap" to peace between Israel and Palestine; Palestinian authority reformed; Prime Minister Abu Mazen elected leader of the PLO; Secretary Powell renewed the peace process
- 2004 - Israel continued to build the Security Fence – a strip about 4050 meters wide that extended from Beit She'an in northern Israel to Arad in the south; Israel agreed to the creation of an independent, peaceful Palestine; the Sharon government announced plans to end all settlements in Gaza; the US "roadmap" was restored following the death of chairman Arafaat

2005 – Withdrawal from Gaza completed; increased cooperation between Sharon and the new PLO leader, Mahmoud Abbas; Sharon resigned from the Likud and called for national elections in early 2006

2006 – Sharon medically incapacitated; Israeli elections produce coalition government; Hamas elected to power in Palestine; all Israeli Palestinian negotiations stopped; major military operations in Southern Lebanon

2007 – Israeli statements that Iran will not be allowed to acquire nuclear weapons; Israeli proclamation that an insurgent victory in Iraq would lead to another holocaust

Jordan

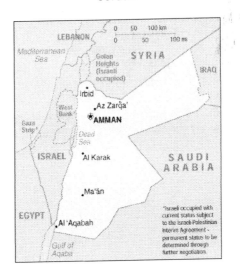

Background:

For most of its history since independence from British administration in 1946, Jordan was ruled by King Hussein (1953-1999). He successfully navigated competing pressures from the major powers (US, USSR, and UK), various Arab states, Israel, and a large internal Palestinian population, through several wars and coup attempts. In 1989 he resumed parliamentary elections and gradually permitted political liberalization; in 1994 a formal peace treaty was signed with Israel. King Abdallah II – the eldest son of King Hussein and Princess Muna – assumed the throne following his father's death in February 1999. Jordan has had a relatively positive relationship with the US. Jordan's new King may be exactly the kind of moderate the US will need in the War on Terrorism

Geography:

Continent: Asia
Total Area: 92,300 sq. km, slightly smaller than Indiana
Terrain: Mostly desert plateau in east, highland area in west; Great Rift Valley separates East and West Banks of the Jordan river

Climate:

    Mostly arid desert; rainy season in west (November to April)

Environmental Issues:

    Limited natural fresh water resources; deforestation; overgrazing; soil erosion

Population:

    5,759,732 (36% under 15 years of age)

Ethnic Groups:

    Arab 98%, Circassian 1%, Armenian 1%

Infant Mortality Rate:

    18.86 deaths/1000 live births

Average Life Expectancy:

    77.88 years

Religions:

    Sunni Muslim 92%, Christian 6% (majority Greek Orthodox, but some Greek Catholics, Roman Catholics, Syrian Orthodox, Coptic Orthodox, Armenian Orthodox, and Protestant denominations), other 2% (several small Shi'a Muslim and Druze populations)

Language:

    Arabic (official), English widely understood among upper and middle classes

Literacy: *(definition: age 15 and over can read and write)*

    Total Population: 91.3%

Male: 95.9%
Female: 86.3%

Government:

Constitutional Monarchy

Capital:

Amman

Economy:

Jordan is a small Arab country with inadequate supplies of water and other natural resources such as oil. The Persian Gulf crisis, which began in August 1990, aggravated Jordan's already serious economic problems, forcing the government to stop most debt payments and suspend rescheduling negotiations. Refugees flooded the country, producing serious balance-of-payments problems, stunting GDP growth, and straining government resources. In an attempt to spur growth, King Abdallah has undertaken limited economic reform, including partial privatization of some state-owned enterprises and Jordan's entry in January 2000 into the World Trade Organization (WTO). Debt, poverty, and unemployment are continuing economic problems

GDP: *(per capita)*

$4,500

Economic Aid

ODA, $500 million

Currency:

Jordanian dinar (JOD)

Televisions:

500,000

Transnational Issues:

Dispute with Israel over the West Bank

Jordan Timeline

1920 - Palestine (including Transjordan) awarded to UK under League of Nations mandate
1922 - British divided Palestine mandate; established semiautonomous Emirate of Transjordan east of Jordan River
1928 - Treaty relaxed British controls over Transjordan; constitution – the Organic Law promulgated
1948-49 - Participated in Arab League invasion of Israel; occupation of West Bank and East Jerusalem; armistice signed in April 1949
1964 - New constitution promulgated; joined Unified Arab Command military alliance
1950 - Annexation of eastern Palestine (West Bank) recognized only by UK and Pakistan; country renamed Hashemite Kingdom of Jordan
1951 - King Abdullah assassinated by Palestinian nationalist
1956 - Jordan avoided major involvement in Suez War
1967 - Lost West Bank, including East Jerusalem, during June War with Israel
1970-71 - Palestinian guerrillas evicted during "Black September;" unrest spread throughout the country
1984 - Parliament reconvened for first time since 1974
1981-88 - Served as land bridge; earning much-needed oil in exchange for supplies to Iraq during Iran-Iraq war
1989 - Direct election of Parliament...first democratically elected body in Jordan's modern era
1990-91 – Domestic pressure kept Jordan neutral during the Gulf War
1994 - Jordan ended State of War with Israel and signed peace treaty
1999 - King Hussein died; Abdullah made King
2001 - Jordan supported US coalition; repeated its long standing condemnation of terrorism
2002 - King Abdullah recruited by President Bush and Secretary Powell to assist moderate Arabs in reestablishing peace in the area

2003 – Jordan supported the US invasion of Iraq "with reservations;" offered its good offices for the US peace proposals regarding Palestine

2004 – Agreement reached under which Baghdad will supply Amman with 50,000 barrels of oil daily through the Irai Port of Al Bakr near Basra; Jordan became the fourth country to have a Free Trade Agreement with the US; Jordan agreed to train Iraqi self-defense forces

2005 – Extensive Jordanian efforts to promote peace between Israel and the Palestinians; Massive terrorist attacks in Amman followed by Jordanian demonstrations against the fundamentalists

2006 -- Considerable crackdown on internal insurgence

2007- Tentative Jordanian support for US objectives in Iraq and Iran

Kuwait

Background:

Kuwait was attacked and overrun by Iraq on August 2, 1990. Following several weeks of aerial bombardment, a US-led UN coalition of 550,000 troops began a ground assault on February 23, 1991 that completely liberated Kuwait in four days. Kuwait has spent more than $5 billion to repair oil infrastructure damaged during 1990-1991. Kuwait is a key part of the American alliance structure in the Gulf. Kuwait provided the US Coalition full support for the invasion of Iraq in 2003. Kuwait was the primary invasion point for all Coalition Forces

Geography:

Continent: Asia
Total Area: 17,820 sq km, slightly smaller than New Jersey
Terrain: Flat to slightly undulating desert plain

Climate:

Dry desert, intensely hot summers; short, cool winters

Environmental Issues:

> Limited natural fresh water resources; some of the world's largest and most sophisticated desalinization facilities provide much of the water; air and water pollution; desertification

Population:

> 2,335,648 (28 % under 15 years of age)

Ethnic Groups:

> Kuwaiti 45%, other Arab 35%, South Asian 9%, Iranian 4%, other 7%

Infant Mortality Rate:

> 10.57 deaths/1,000 live births

Average Life Expectancy:

> 76.65 years

Religions:

> Muslim 85% (Sunni 70%, Shi'a 30%), Christian, Hindu, Parsi, and other 15%

Language:

> Arabic (official), English widely spoken

Literacy: *(definition: age 15 and older can read and write)*

> Total population: 83.5%
> Male: 85.1%
> Female: 81.7%

Government:

> Nominal constitutional monarchy

Capital:

> Kuwait City

Economy:

> Kuwait is a small, relatively open economy with proven crude oil reserves of about 94 billion barrels – 10% of world reserves. Petroleum accounts for nearly half of GDP, 90% of export revenues, and 75% of government income. Kuwait's climate limits agricultural development. Consequently, with the exception of fish, it depends almost entirely on food imports. About 75% of potable water must be distilled or imported. Kuwait continues its discussions with foreign oil companies to develop fields in the northern part of the country

GDP: *(per capita)*

> $ 21,300

Economic Aid

> N/A

Currency:

> Kuwaiti dinal (KWD)

Televisions:

> 875,000

Transnational Issues:

> In November 1994, Iraq formally accepted the UN-demarcated border with Kuwait that had been spelled out in Security Council Resolutions 687 (1991), 773 (1993), and 883 (1993); this formally ended earlier claims to Kuwait and to Bublyan and Warbah islands

Kuwait Timeline

1899 - Kuwait signed comprehensive agreement with UK, but remained under nominal Turkish sovereignty until end of World War I
1913 - Boundary with Iraq defined by Anglo-Turkish Convention
1922 - Boundary with Saudi Arabia agreed upon; along with creation of Kuwait-Saudi neutral zone
1934 - Oil exploitation concession granted to British-American-owned Kuwait Oil Company; Anglo-Yemeni Treaty of Sanaa set stage for future existence of two independent nations in southwest Arabi
1938 - Oil discovered; oilfield development delayed by World War II
1946 - Oil export began
1950 - First seawater desalination plant built near the capital
1961 - Kuwait achieved independence ending 1899 agreement with UK; Iraq claimed sovereignty over the new state; British responded by sending troops
1969 - Kuwait and Saudi Arabia partitioned their Neutral Zone; oil production shared with Saudi Arabia
1973 - Armed clashes along border with Iraq
1976 - Government assumed control of Kuwait Oil Company
1981 - Oil sector reorganized under state-owned Kuwait Petroleum Corp; Kuwait led in forming six-country Gulf Cooperation Council (GCC)
1986 - National Assembly dissolved
1987 - Kuwaiti tankers re-registered under Western flags for protection against Iranian attacks
1988 - Cease-fire between Iran and Iraq ended Iranian threat to Kuwait
1990 - Iraq invaded Kuwait; annexed it as Iraq's 19th province
1991 - Coalition forces ousted Iraqis; Al-Sabah family restored to power
1992 - Election held for National Assembly
1994 - Iraq formally accepted UN-demarcated border with Kuwait
2001 - Kuwait condemned the Taliban and pledged total support for the US coalition
2002 - The Emir condemned Prime Minister Sharon but restated Kuwaiti support for the US
2003 - Kuwait became America's staunchest Arab ally in toppling the Iraqi regime
2004 - Kuwait offered $500 million in addition to the $1 billion already spent at the Iraq Donor Conference
2005 – Local elections held; women allowed to vote
2007 – Continued support for US efforts in Iraq

Pakistan

Background:

The separation in 1947 of British India into the Muslim state of Pakistan (with two sections West and East) and largely Hindu India was never satisfactorily resolved. A third war between these countries in 1971 resulted in East Pakistan seceding and becoming the separate nation of Bangladesh. A dispute over the state of Kashmir is ongoing. In response to Indian nuclear weapons testing, Pakistan conducted its own tests in 1998. President Musharraf courageously sided with the US allowing Pakistan to become a base for military action against Afghanistan in 2001. General Powell's visit to Islamabad in Oct. 2001 illustrated Washington's vital goal of keeping the peace between India and Pakistan. Pakistan's problems are compounded by millions of refugees, most of whom are fundamentalists

Geography:

Continent: Asia
Total Area: 803,940 sq km, slightly less than twice the size of California
Terrain: Flat Indus plain in east; mountains in north and northwest; Balochistan plateau in west

Climate:

> Mostly hot, dry desert; temperate in northwest; arctic in north

Environmental Issues:

> Water pollution from raw sewage, industrial wastes, and agricultural runoff; limited natural fresh water resources; a majority of the population does not have access to potable water; deforestation; soil erosion; desertification

Population:

> 162,419,946 (40 % under 15 years of age)

Ethnic Groups:

> Punjab, Sindhi, Pashtun (Pathan), Baloch, Muhajir (immigrants from India at the time of partition and their descendants)

Infant Mortality Rate:

> 76.53 deaths/1,000 live births

Average Life Expectancy:

> 62.2 years

Religions:

> Muslim 97% (Sunni 77%, Shi'a 20%), Christian, Hindu, and other 3%

Language:

> Punjab 48%, Sindhi 12%, Siraki (a Punjabi variant), 10% Pashtu 8%, Urdu (official) 8%, Balochi 3%, Hindko 2%, Brahue 1%, English (official and lingua franca of Pakistani elite and most government ministries), Burushaski, and other 8%

Literacy: *(definition: age 15 and older can read and write)*

    Total population: 45.7%
    Males: 59.8%
    Females: 30.6%

Government:

    Military Dictatorship

Capital:

    Islamabad

Economy:

    Pakistan is a poor, heavily populated country, suffering from internal political disputes, lack of foreign investment, and a costly confrontation with neighboring India. Pakistan's economic outlook continues to be marred by its weak foreign exchange position, which relies on international creditors for hard currency inflows. The Musharraf government will face an estimated $21 bill in foreign debt coming due in 2000-2003, despite having rescheduled nearly $2 billion in debt with Paris Club members. Foreign loans and grants provide approximately 25% of government revenue, but debt service obligations total nearly 50% of government expenditure

GDP: *(per capita)*

    $2,200

Economic Aid

    Recipient: $2.4 billion

Currency:

    Pakistani rupee (PKR)

Televisions:

> 3.1 million

Transnational Issues:

> Key transit area for Southwest Asian heroin moving to Western markets; narcotics still move from Afghanistan into Balochistan Province

Pakistan Timeline

1947 - Pakistan gained independence
1948 - Muhammad Ali Jinnah, father of Pakistan, died; Indo-Pak fighting broke out over Kashmir
1949 - UN brokered cease-fire
1956 - First Constitution adopted; became "Islamic Republic"
1958 - Martial Law declared
1959 - Military government shifted capital from Karachi to Rawalpindi
1962 - Martial law ended; new constitution promulgated
1963 - Zulifikar Ali Bhutto became foreign minister
1965 - First presidential election; war over Kashmir
1966 - Tashkent Agreement ended 1965 war with India
1969 - Second period of martial law declared; 1963 constitution suspended
1970 - Martial law ended; legal elections held; Islamabad became new capital
1971 - E. Pakistan (now Bangladesh) declared independence; civil war ensued; India intervened in E. Pakistan
1973 - New Constitution promulgated; Zulfikar Bhutto became Prime Minister
1974 - Pakistan officially recognized Bangladesh
1977 - Martial law established; 1973 constitution suspended; Bhutto overthrown in coup led by Army Commander in Chief al-Haq
1979 - Bhutto executed; U.S. Embassy in Islamabad stormed and burned by angry mobs supporting Ayatollah Khomeini in Iran
1981 - India deployed troops to Siachen Glacier north of contested Jammu Kashmir
1984 - Pakistan deployed troops to Siachen Glacier; first U.S. F-16 fighters delivered to Pakistan
1985 - Martial law ended; 1973 constitution amended and reinstated

1988 - Benazir Bhutto named PM; Ishaq Khan became President
1990 - Border crisis; Indo-Pak military deployed to Line of Control in Kashmir; President Khan dismissed PM Bhutto and National Assembly; Nawaz Sharif elected as new PM; US suspended all military aid to Pakistan
1991 - Pakistan deployed 10,000 troops to Saudi Arabia to provide non-combat support to coalition
1993 - Pakistan deployed troops to Somalia in support of United Nations Operations Somalia (UNOSOM); US imposed sanctions on Pakistan and China for violation of international arms control agreements
1996 - President Leghari dissolved National Assembly and Bhutto government, installed caretaker government
1997 - Free elections held; Nawaz Sharif re-elected PM
1998 - Rafiq Tarar elected President in February; in May, India and Pakistan conducted nuclear tests, removed shroud of nuclear ambiguity from sub-continent; US and other countries imposed economic sanctions against both countries; Pakistan was hardest hit and struggled on the verge of economic collapse; relations with regional neighbors remained tense
2000 - Military coup; Musharraf installed as "interim President"
2001 - Pakistan supported the US coalition and allowed the US to use Pakistani bases and full use of Pakistani airspace; the US lifted all sanctions against Pakistan and increased its foreign aid; US called for calm between India and Pakistan concerning Kashmir
2002 – Pakistan and India mobilized forces along opposite sides of the Kashmir frontier; Pakistan assisted the US in the hunt for Osama bin Laden; President Musharraf "reelected" for five years in a national referendum; US forces "secretly" moved into Pakistan in pursuit of Al Qaeda
2003 - Continued support for US attacks on Al Qaeda; the US 82nd Airborne Division moved freely throughout the Afghan/Pakistani border area
2004 - President Musharraf stated: "We are gaining ground day-by-day against terrorists …and in this connection, Pakistan has close cooperation with the Coalition forces and the US;" Pakistan broadly accepted India's 12-point peace proposal over the disputed territory of Kashmir; IMF approved disbursement of $250 million to Pakistan in line with the Poverty Reduction and Growth Facility (PRFG) arrangement

2005 – Continued Pakistani success in capturing and controlling Al Qaeda terrorists
2006 – Increased US – Pakistani attacks on Al Qaeda in Western Pakistan
2007- Continued US support for President Musharraf

Saudi Arabia

Background:

In 1902, Abdul al-Aziz Ibn Saud captured Riyadh and set out on a 30-year campaign to unify the Arabian Peninsula. In the 1930s, the discovery of oil transformed the country. Following Iraq's invasion of Kuwait in 1990, Saudi Arabia accepted the Kuwaiti royal family and 400,000 refugees while allowing Western and Arab troops to deploy on its soil for the liberation of Kuwait the following year. A burgeoning population, aquifer depletion, and an economy largely dependent on petroleum output and prices are all major governmental concerns. Saudi Arabia remains America's most important ally in the region

Geography:

Continent: Asia
Total Area: 1,960,582 sq km, slightly more than one-fifth the size of the US Terrain: Mostly uninhabited, sandy desert

Climate:

Harsh, dry desert with great extremes of temperature

Environmental Issues:

> Desertification; depletion of underground water resources; the lack of perennial rivers or permanent water bodies has prompted the development of extensive seawater desalination facilities; coastal pollution from oil spills

Population:

> 26,417,599 (42% under 15 years of age)

Ethnic Groups:

> Arab 90%, Afro-Asian 10%

Infant Mortality Rate:

> 47.94 deaths/1,000 live births

Average Life Expectancy:

> 68.73 years

Religions:

> Muslim 100%

Language:

> Arabic

Literacy: *(definition: age 15 and older can read and write)*

> Total population: 78.8%
> Male: 84.7%
> Female: 70.8%

Government:

> Monarchy

Capital:

> Riyadh

Economy:

> This is an oil-based economy with strong government controls over major economic activities. Saudi Arabia has the largest reserves of petroleum in the world (26% of the proven reserves), ranks as the largest exporter of petroleum, and plays a leading role in OPEC. The petroleum sector accounts for roughly 75% of budget revenues, 40% of GDP, and 90% of export earnings. About 35% of GDP comes from the private sector. Roughly 5 million foreign workers play an important role in the Saudi economy in the oil and service sectors

GDP: *(per capita)*

> $12,000

Economic Aid

> Donor: Pledged $100 million in 1993 to fund reconstruction of Lebanon; since 1993, Saudi Arabia has committed $208 million for assistance to the Palestinians including the families of suicide bombers

Currency:

> Saudi riyal (SAR)

Televisions:

> 5.1 million

Transnational Issues:

> Death penalty for traffickers, increasing consumption of heroin and cocaine

Saudi Arabia Timeline

1750 -1900 - Saudi rulers contended with Egypt, Ottoman Turks, and other Arabian families for control over the peninsula
1913 - British arranged Turks ouster from Al Hasa (present day Eastern Province)
1922 - Boundary with Iraq and Kuwait agreed upon, along with creation of the Neutral Zone
1924-27 - 'Abdul' Aziz conquered Hejaz and most of Asir and became King of Hejaz and Nadj
1932 - Abdul' Aziz created the Kingdom of Saudi Arabia
1933 - Oil concession agreement signed with Standard Oil Company of California; renamed Armaco
1938 - Discovery of oil near Dhahran
1947-50 - Construction of Trans- Arabian Pipeline (Tapline) to the Mediterranean; via Jordan, Syria, and Lebanon
1953 - King 'Abdul' Aziz died; succeeded by his eldest son
1955 - UK, acting on behalf of Abu Dhabi, unilaterally defined Saudi Arabia's Eastern boundaries
1960 - OPEC formed with Saudi Arabia, Iran, Iraq, Kuwait, and Venezuela
1964 - King Sa'ud relinquished throne to Crown Prince Faysal
1967 - Saudi Arabia and UAR (Egypt) ended confrontation in Yemen civil war
1968 - Offshore boundary with Iran delimited by treaty
1973 - Following US support of Israel in October War, Saudis led Arab oil boycott of the US
1975 - King Faysal assassinated; Khalid became King
1977 - Diplomatic relation broken with Egypt over Camp David accords; relations restored in 1987
1988 - King Khalid died; brother Fahd became King; Saudis played major role in bringing cease-fire to Iran-Iraq War
1990-91 - Coalition forces invited to use Saudi bases during Gulf War; Saudi Arabia was a major player in ousting Iraq from Kuwait
2001 - Crown Prince Abdullah effectively replaced King Fahd as the ruler of the Kingdom; Saudi Arabia supported the anti-Taliban coalition; demanded coalition help with Palestinian demands for independence
2002 - The Saudi Kingdom denounced extremism within Islam; the Kingdom proposed a regional peace settlement based on total Arab recognition of Israel in exchange for Israeli return to the pre-1967 borders; the Crown Prince visited President Bush in Crawford, Texas;

both "hinted" about a "deal;" the Saudis would control Arafat and the US would subdue Sharon

2003 - Full Saudi cooperation with the US/UK invasion of Iraq

2004 - Saudi Arabia pledged $1 billion for Iraq, half in loans through 2007, at the Iraq Donor Conference; Prince Saud Al-Faisal agreed to reduce some of the $24 billion it is owed by Iraq; the Kingdom experienced massive increases in Al Qaeda sponsored terrorist attacks; the Crown Prince proclaimed closer ties with the US in its war against terrorists

2005 – Local elections held; women allowed to vote; Saudi promises to increase oil production

2006 – Substantial increases in oil prices

2007- Continued Saudi support for US operations in Iraq; ineffective Saudi efforts to bring stability to Lebanon

Somalia

Background:

Asaid Barre regime was ousted in January 1991; turmoil, factional fighting, and anarchy followed for nine years. Beginning in 1993, a two-year UN humanitarian effort (primarily in the south) was able to alleviate famine conditions, but when the UN withdrew in 1995, having suffered significant casualties, order still had not been restored. Numerous warlords and factions are still fighting for control of Mogadishu and the other southern regions. Somalia is known to have several al-Qaeda cells and base camps. Somalia is clearly on President Bush's list of nations which host terrorists

Geography:

Continent: Africa
Total Area: 637,657 sq km, slightly smaller than Texas
Terrain: Mostly flat to undulating plateau rising to hills in north

Climate:

Principally desert; December to February – northeast monsoon, moderate temperatures in north and very hot in south; May to October – southwest monsoon, torrid in the north and hot in the south, irregular rainfall, hot and humid periods (tangambill) between monsoons

Environmental Issues:

Famine; use of contaminated water contributes to human health problems; deforestation; overgrazing; soil erosion; desertification

Population:

8,591,629 (45% under 15 years of age)

Ethnic Groups:

Somali 85% / 15% made up of five Somali Clan Groups: Dir, Issaq, Darod, Hawiye, Digil

Infant Mortality Rate:

120.34 deaths/1,000 live births

Average Life Expectancy:

47.34 years

Religions:

Sunni Muslim

Language:

Somali (official), Arabic, Italian, English

Literacy: *(definition: age 15 and older can read and write)*

Total population: 37.8%
Male: 49.7%
Female: 25.8%

Government:

    Dysfunctional

Capital:

    Mogadishu

Economy:

    One of the world's poorest and least developed countries, Somalia has few resources. Moreover, much of the economy has been devastated by the civil war. Agriculture is the most important sector, with livestock accounting for about 40% of GDP and about 65% of export earnings. Nomads and semi-nomads, who are dependent upon livestock for their livelihood, make up a large portion of the population; all livestock exports were banned in 2001 because of Rift Valley fever which can be fatal to humans

GDP: *(per capita)*

    $ 600

Economic Aid

    Recipient: $60 million

Currency:

    Somali shilling

Televisions:

    135,000

Military:

    Thirty factions and clans maintain independent militias, and the Somaliland and Puntland regional government maintain their own security and police forces

Transnational Issues:

Most of the southern half of the boundary with Ethiopia is a provisional administrative line; territorial dispute with Ethiopia over Ogaden

Somalia Timeline

1848 - British returned Ogaden to Ethiopia
1935 - Italy invaded Ethiopia
1885-1960 – Colonies separated: French Somaliland, British Somaliland, the Ogaden District, and the Northern Frontier District
1941 - Britain seized Ogaden region
1949 – Somalia was made a trust territory under Italian rule
1956 - Southern Somalia held first elections
1960 - Single state emerged composed of Italian Somalia and British Somaliland; democracy established
1969 - Siad Barre seized power in coup
1977 - Somalia declared war on Ethiopia to gain control of Ogaden
1979 - Constitution ratified
1981 - Somali National Movement began as a guerrilla movement
1991 - Collapse of state, Siad Barre fled to Southern Somalia
1992 - Siad Barre left Somalia; US intervened to restore order
1993 - US withdrawal began in December
1995 - Withdrawal of international forces
2001 - Somalia condemned terrorism; proclaimed no terrorist bases
2002 - US forces dispatched to Kenya
2003 - US military action against Al Qaeda bases
2004 - Widespread economic and political disorder
2005 - US forces continued to track terrorist's cells
2007 – No effective national government; considerable Al Qaeda activity

Sudan

Background:

Military dictatorships promulgating an Islamic government have run the country since independence from the UK in 1956. Over the past two decades, a civil war pitting black Christians and animists in the south against the Arab-Muslims of the north has cost at least 1.5 million lives in war and famine related deaths, as well as the displacement of millions of others. The Sudan is a prime target in the war on terrorism. The Sudan allowed Osama bin Laden to train terrorists throughout the North

Geography:

Continent: Africa
Total Area: 2,505,810 sq km, slightly more than one-quarter the size of the US

Terrain:

Generally flat, featureless plain; mountains in east and west

Climate:

> Tropical in south; arid desert in north; rainy season (April to October)

Environmental Issues:

> Inadequate supplies of potable water; wildlife populations threatened by excessive hunting; soil erosion; desertification

Population:

> 40,187,486 (45% under 15 years of age)

Ethnic Groups:

> Black 52%, Arab 39%, Beja 6%, foreigners 2%, other 1%

Infant Mortality Rate:

> 65.59 deaths/1,000 live births

Average Life Expectancy:

> 57.73 years

Religions:

> Sunni Muslim 70% (in north), indigenous beliefs 25%, Christian 5% (mostly in south and Khartoum)

Language:

> Arabic (official), Nubian, Ta Bedawie, diverse dialects of Nilotic, Nio-Hamitic, Sudanic languages, English

Literacy: *(definition: age 15 and older can read and write)*

> Total population: 61.1%
> Male: 71.8%
> Female: 50.5%

Government:

> Transitional ruling military junta took power in 1989; government dominated by members of Sudan's National Islamic Front (NIF), a fundamentalist political organization, which uses the National Congress Party (NCP) as its legal front

Capital:

> Khartoum

Economy:

> Sudan is buffeted by civil war, chronic instability, adverse weather, weak world agricultural prices, a drop in foreign aid, and counterproductive economic policies. Despite its many infrastructure problems, Sudan's increased oil production, the return of regular rainfall, and recent investments in irrigation schemes should allow the country to achieve economic growth of 6% in 2002

GDP: *(per capita)*

> $1,900

Economic Aid

> Recipient: $187 million

Currency:

> Sudanese dinar (SDD)

Televisions:

> 2.38 million

Transnational Issues:

Administrative boundary with Kenya does not coincide with international boundary; Egypt asserts its claim to the "Hala'b Triangle," a barren area of 20,580 sq km under partial Sudanese administration that is defined by an administrative boundary which supersedes the treaty boundary of 1899

Sudan Timeline

1956 - Sudan became an independent republic on New Years Day
1958 - Umma Party won majority in first national elections. Abdullah Khalil elected prime minister; General Ibrahim Abboud seized power in military coup
1959 - Abboud assumed supreme power
1964 - Abboud yeilded power in wake of mass rioting in Khartoum; Al Khatim al Khalifa named prime minister; Abboud fled the country
1965 - National elections were held for the National Assembly; Umma Party won largest number of seats; Mahgoub elected Prime Minister
1966 - Mahgoub lost vote of confidence in National Assembly; Sadiq al Mahdi became new Prime Minister
1969 - National Assembly dissolved; new elections held; Mahgoub returned as prime minister; General Jaafar Muhammad Numayri led army back into power in coup d'etat; Abubakr Awadullah became Prime Minister; all opposition parties outlawed
1970 - Rebellion by Ansar, a religious sect, was put down; their leader, the mahdi, was killed
1971 - Sudan Socialist Party founded as sole political party
1973 - US Ambassador Cleo Noel and his deputy Curtis Moore were assassinated by Black September group of Palestinian terrorists; new constitution was promulgated
1981 - National Assembly was dissolved
1983 - Numayri re-elected; Sharia (Islamic Law) introduced; civil war reignited
1986 - Umma Party (UP) and the Democratic Unionist Party (DUP) gained majority of seats in National Assembly; power handed over to civilian government headed by the Umma Party's Sadiq al-Mahdi
1988 - Sadiq al-Mahdi resigned to make way for a government of national reconciliation

1989 - A new coalition government was formed in March, composed of the UP, the DUP, and representatives of unions and southern parties; the army took power in coup led by BG Omar Hassan Ahmad al-Bashir

1990 - Heavy fighting erupted in the south. Africa Watch estimated 500,000 people died in the previous four years as a result of the war and famine; government survived two attempted coups

1991 - Ruling military council passed a decree converting the country into a federal system; Islamic law was affirmed as national law

1993 - Sudan placed on US State-sponsored terrorism list

1996 - UN passed UNSCR 1044, calling for Sudan to cease support to terrorism; US closed embassy

2001 - Sudan condemned terrorism; proclaimed no terrorist bases in Sudan

2003 - US Special Forces reported to be on reconnaissance missions in Sudan

2004 - The US extended sanctions against Sudan because of its support for terrorists

2005 - Sudan was identified by President Bush as a threat to US national security

2006 – US brokered peace Drafur; famine in the South; continued support for Al Qaeda by the Khartoum government

2007- Collapse of the peace agreement; continued Civil War

Syria

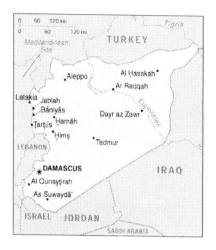

Background:

Following the breakup of the Ottoman Empire during World War I, Syria was administered by the French until independence in 1946. In the 1967 Arab-Israeli War, Syria lost the Golan Heights to Israel. Since 1976, Syrian troops have been stationed in Lebanon, ostensibly in a peacekeeping capacity. In recent years, Syria and Israel have held peace talks over the return of the Golan Heights with no success. Syria is on the American list of nations which harbor and sponsor terrorism. The Syrian occupation of Lebanon has strained Syrian relations with the West. The ascension to power of President Assad's son, Bashar al-Asad, may provide an opening for improved relations with the US. Syria is the home base of two of the world's most prominent terrorist organizations – the Hamas and Hizballah. The US Coalition may face one of its greatest challenges with Syria – how to manage a regime allegedly supporting the Coalition while at the same time harboring terrorists

Geography:

Total Area: 185,180 sq. km., slightly larger than North Dakota
Terrain: Primarily semiarid and desert plateau; narrow coastal plains; mountains in west

Climate:

Mostly desert; hot, dry, sunny summers (June to August) and mild, rainy winters (December to February) along coast; cold weather with snow or sleet periodically hitting Damascus

Environmental Issues:

Deforestation; overgrazing; soil erosion; desertification; water pollution from dumping of raw sewage and wastes from petroleum refining; inadequate supplies of potable water

Population:

18,448,752 (39% under 15 years of age)

Ethnic Groups:

Arab 90.3%, Kurds, Armenians, and other 9.7%

Infant Mortality Rate:

31.67 deaths/1,000 live births

Average Life Expectancy:

69.39 years

Religions:

Sunni Muslim 74%, Alawite, Druze, and other Muslim sects 16%, Christian (various sects) 10%, Jewish (tiny communities in Damascus, Al Qamishli, and Aleppo)

Language:

Arabic (official); Kurdish, Armenian, Aramaic, Circassian widely understood; French, English somewhat understood

Literacy: *(definition: age 15 and older can read and write)*

    Total population: 76.9%
    Male: 89.7%
    Female: 64%

Government:

    Presidential/Military Dictatorship

Capital:

    Damascus

Economy:

    Syria's predominantly state controlled economy is on a shaky footing because of Damascus' failure to implement extensive economic reform. The dominant agricultural sector remains underdeveloped, with roughly 80% of agricultural land still dependent on rainfed sources. Oil production is leveling off, and the efforts of the non-oil sector to penetrate international markets have fallen short. Syria's inadequate infrastructure, outmoded technological base, and weak educational system make it vulnerable to future shocks and hamper competition with neighbors such as Jordan and Israel

GDP: *(per capita)*

    $3,400

Economic Aid:

    $180 million

Currency:

    Syrian pound (SYP)

Televisions:

    1.05 million

Transnational Issues:

    A transit point for opiates and hashish bound for regional and Western markets

Syria Timeline

- 1922 - French mandate over Syria declared by the League of Nations 1946 - British left Syria; Syria became both a republic and a charter member of the United Nations
- 1963 - Ba'ath party came to power, Syria began to stabilize
- 1970 - Hafez al-Assad nominated President and remained in office until his death in June 2000
- 1974 – War with Israel
- 1991 - Syria sent troops to fight Iraq during Desert Storm
- 2000 - President Assad died and was replaced by his son Bashar
- 2001 - Syria condemned terrorism; proclaimed no terrorist bases in Syria
- 2002 - Syria continued to support Hamas and other terrorist groups throughout the Middle East
- 2003 - President Al Assad supported Iraq; provided safe haven for many of Saddam Hussein's lieutenants; warned by Secretaries Powell and Rumsfeld to cooperate with the US Coalition or face "serious consequences"
- 2004 - Syria condemned by the US for pursuing weapons of mass destruction; US accused Syria of sponsoring terrorism, occupying Lebanon, and not doing enough to secure its border with Iraq
- 2005 – Total Syrian withdrawal from Lebanon
- 2007 – Major US – Iraqi efforts to close the Syrian border; continued Syrian support for the Iraqi insurgence

Tajikistan

Background:

Tajikistan has experienced three changes in government and a five-year civil war since it gained independence in 1991 from the USSR. A peace agreement among rival factions was signed in 1997, and implementation reportedly completed by late 1999. Part of the agreement required the legalization of opposition political parties prior to the 1999 elections, which occurred, but such parties have made little progress in successful participation in government. Random criminal and political violence in the country remains. Tajikistan has allowed the US to fly over its territory in the War on Terrorism

Geography:

Continent: Asia
Total Area: 143,100 sq km, slightly smaller than Wisconsin
Terrain: Pamir and Alay mountains dominate landscape; western Fergana Valley in north, Kofamihon and Vahkish Valley in southwest

Climate:

Midlatitude continental, hot summers, mild winters; semiarid to polar in Pamir Mountains

Environmental Issues:

    Inadequate sanitation facilities; increasing levels of soil salinity; industrial pollution; excessive pesticides; part of the basin of the shrinking Aral Sea suffers from severe over utilization of available water for irrigation and associated pollution

Population:

    7,163,506 (40% under 15 years of age)

Ethnic Groups:

    Tajik 64.9%, Uzbek 25%, Russian 3.5% (declining because of emigration), other 6.6%

Infant Mortality Rate:

    113.43 deaths/1,000 live births

Average Life Expectancy:

    64.18 years

Religions:

    Sunni Muslim 85%, Shi'a Muslim 5%

Language:

    Tajik (official), Russian widely used in government and business

Literacy: *(definition: age 15 and older can read and write)*

    Total population: 99.4%
    Male: 99%
    Female: 99.1%

Government:

> Dictatorship

Capital:

> Dushanbe

Economy:

> Tajikistan has the lowest per capita GDP among the 15 former Soviet republics. Cotton is the most important crop. Mineral resources, varied but limited in amount, include silver, gold, uranium, and tungsten. Industry consists only of a large aluminum plant, hydropower facilities, and small obsolete factories mostly in light industry and food processing. The Tajikistani economy has been gravely weakened by six years of civil conflict and by the loss of subsidies from Moscow and of markets for its products. Most of its people live in abject poverty. Tajikistan depends on aid from Russia and Uzbekistan and on international humanitarian assistance for much of its basic subsistence needs

GDP: *(per capita)*

> $1100

Economic Aid

> Recipient: $60.7 million

Currency:

> Sonomi (TJS)

Televisions:

> 860,000

Transnational Issues:

> Major transshipment zone for heroin and opiates from Afghanistan going to Russia and Western Europe; limited illicit cultivation of cannabis, mostly for domestic consumption

Tajikistan Timeline

Late 1800s to Early 1900s - Russians conquered and colonized the area which now makes up Tajikistan
1924 - Tajikistan formed as an autonomous region within the Uzbek Soviet Socialist Republic
1929 - The Tajik Soviet Socialist Republic was formed
1991 - Tajikistan declared its independence
1993 - Tajikistan began to form its own armed forces
1996 - Civil War
1997 - The Moscow Peace Accord was signed, officially ending the Civil War in June
2001 - Tajikistan supported the US Coalition; allowed air corridors for US military aircraft
2002 - Secretary Rumsfeld announced continued cooperation between the US and Tajikistan
2003 - Tajikistan supported the US invasion of Iraq
2004 - American forces continued to use bases in Tajikistan to help fight the war in Afghanistan; Constitution amended to allow President Imomali Rakhmonov to run for two more seven-year terms
2005 - Tajikistan and the US continued military-technical information exchange
2007 – US military aid increased

Turkey

Background:

Turkey was created in 1923 from the Turkish remnants of the Ottoman Empire. Soon thereafter the country instituted secular laws to replace traditional religious fiats. In 1945 Turkey joined the UN and in 1952 it became a member of NATO. Turkey occupied the northern portion of Cyprus in 1974 to prevent a Greek takeover of the island; relations between the two countries remain strained. Periodic military offensives against Kurdish separatists have dislocated part of the population in southeast Turkey and have drawn international condemnation. Turkey has consistently been one of America's most faithful allies in the region although Turkey refused to allow US Forces to attack Iraq from its territory in 2003.

Geography:

Continent: Asia
Total Area: 780,000 sq km, slightly larger than Texas
Terrain: Mostly mountains; narrow coastal plain; high central plateau (Anatolia)

Climate:

> Temperate; hot, dry summers with mild, wet winters; harsher in interior

Environmental Issues:

> Water pollution from dumping of chemicals and detergents; air pollution, particularly in urban areas; deforestation; concern for oil spills from increasing Bosporus ship traffic

Population:

> 69,660,559 (27.2 % under15 years of age)

Ethnic Groups:

> Turkish 80%, Kurdish 20%]

Infant Mortality Rate:

> 44.2 deaths/1,000 live births

Average Life Expectancy:

> 71.8 years

Religions:

> Muslims 99.8% (mostly Sunni), other .2% (Christians and Jews)

Language:

> Turkish (official), Kurdish, Arabic, Armenian, Greek

Literacy: *(definition: age 15 and over can read and write)*

> Total population: 86.5%
> Male: 94%
> Female: 78.7%

Government:

> Republican parliamentary democracy

Capital:

> Ankara

Economy:

> Turkey's dynamic economy is a complex mix of modern industry and commerce along with traditional agriculture that still accounts for nearly 40% of employment. It has a strong and rapidly growing private sector, yet the state still plays a major role in basic industry, banking, transport, and communication. Real GNP growth has exceeded 6% in most years, but this strong expansion was interrupted by sharp declines in output in 1994 and 1999. Meanwhile the public sector fiscal deficit has regularly exceeded 10% of GDP- due in large part to the huge burden of interest payments, which now account for more than 40% of central government spending- while inflation has remained in the high double digit range. Perhaps because of these problems, foreign direct investment in Turkey remains low- less than $1 billion annually. The country experienced a financial crisis in late 2000, including sharp drops in the stock market and foreign exchange reserves, but is recovering rapidly, thanks to additional IMF support and the government's commitment to a specific timetable of economic reforms

GDP: *(per capita)*

> $7,400

Economic Aid

> Recipient: 635 million

Currency:

> Turkish lira (TRL)

Televisions:

    20.9 million

Military:

    Turkey hosts the US Sixth Fleet and US Air Force (European Command)

Transnational Issues:

    Key transit route for Southwest Asian heroin to Western Europe and – to a far lesser extent the US – via air, land, and sea routes; major Turkish, Iranian, and other international trafficking organizations operate out of Istanbul; laboratories to convert imported morphine base into heroin are in remote regions of Turkey as well as near Istanbul; government maintains strict controls over areas of legal opium poppy cultivation and output of poppy straw concentrate

Turkey Timeline

1923 - Assembly declared Turkey a republic and Demal Ataturk as president
1925 - Adoption of Gregorian calender; prohibition of the fez
1928 - Turkey became secular: clause retaining Islam as state religion removed from constitution
1938 - President Ataturk died, succeeded by Ismet Inonu
1945 - Turkey entered war on side of Allies against Germany; joined United Nations
1952 - Turkey abandoned Ataturk's neutralist policy and joined NATO
1960 - Army coup against ruling Democratic Party
1961 - New constitution established two-chamber parliament
1963 - Association agreement signed with European Economic Community (EEC)
1965 - Suleyman Demirel became Prime Minister - a position he was to hold seven times
1971 - Army forced Demirel's resignation after spiral of political violence
1974 - Turkish troops invaded northern Cyprus
1978 - US trade embargo resulting from invasion lifted

- 1980 - Military coup followed political deadlock and civil unrest; imposition of martial law
- 1982 - New constitution created seven-year presidency, and reduced parliament to single house
- 1990 - Turkey allowed US-led coalition against Iraq to launch air strikes from Turkish bases
- 1992 - 20,000 Turkish troops entered Kurdish safe havens in Iraq in anti PKK operation; Turkey joined Black Sea alliance
- 1995 - Major military offensive launched against the Kurds in northern Iraq, involved some 35,000 Turkish troops
- 1998 - January - Welfare Party - the largest in parliament – banned; Yelmaz resigned amid corruption allegations, replaced by Bulent
- 1999 - February - PKK leader Abdullah Ocalan captured in Kenya; July Ocalan received death sentence
- 2000 - Ahmet Necdet Sezer replaced Suleyman Demirel as president 2001 - Turkey became the first Muslim country to send troops to Afghanistan to fight the Taliban; joined the US peacekeeping force in the post-Taliban regime
- 2002 - Turkey deployed peacekeeping forces to Kabal; US Special Forces sent to Georgia along the Turkish frontier
- 2003 - Turkey did not allow US Forces to cross its border for the Coalition attack on Iraq but did allow the US to us Turkish airspace for missile attacks
- 2004 - Turkey contributed 4000 troops to the international force in Afghanistan
- 2005 - Turkey offered to deploy 8000 troops to Iraq; US continued to support the admission of Turkey to the EU
- 2006 – Turkish EU admission blocked by Germany and France
- 2007- Increased Turkish concern about the growing independence of "Kurdistan"

Turkmenistan

Background:

Annexed by Russia between 1865 and 1885, Turkmenistan became a Soviet republic in 1925. It achieved its independence upon the dissolution of the USSR in 1991. President Niyazov retains absolute control over the country and opposition is not tolerated. Extensive hydrocarbon/natural gas reserves could prove a boon to this underdeveloped country if extraction and delivery projects can be worked out. Turkmenistan allowed the US military to use its air space for the coalition attacks on Afghanistan in 2001. Turkmenistan is exactly the kind of ally the US feels uncomfortable with regarding the question of human rights but exactly the kind of ally America will need in the War on Terrorism

Geography:

Total Area: 488,100 sq. km, slightly larger than California
Terrain: Flat-to-rolling sandy desert with dunes rising to mountains in the south; low mountains along border with Iran; borders Caspian Sea in west

Climate:

> Subtropical desert

Environmental Issues:

> Contamination of soil and groundwater with agricultural chemicals, pesticides; salination, water-logging of soil due to poor irrigation methods; Caspian Sea pollution; diversion of a large share of the flow of the Samu Darya into irrigation contributes to the river's inability to replenish the Aral Sea; desertification

Population:

> 4,952,081 (37% under 15 years of age)

Ethnic Groups:

> Turkmen 77%, Uzbek 9.2%, Russian 6.7%, Kazakah 2%, Other 5.1%

Infant Mortality Rate:

> 73.25 deaths/1,000 live births

Average Life Expectancy:

> 61 years

Religions:

> Muslim 89%, Eastern Orthodox 9%, unknown 2%

Language:

> Turkmen 72%, Russian 12%, Uzbek 9%, other 7%.

Literacy: *(definition: age 15 and older can read and write)*

> Total population: 98%
> Male: 99%

Female: 97%

Government:

Presidential Dictatorship

Capital:

Ashgabat

Economy:

Turkmenistan is a largely desert country with intensive agriculture in oases and huge gas (fifth largest reserves in the world) and oil resources. One-half of its irrigated land is planted in cotton, making it the world's tenth largest producer. Until the end of 1993, Turkmenistan had experienced less economic disruption than the other former Soviet states because its economy received a boost from higher prices for oil and gas and a sharp increase in hard currency earnings. In 1994, Russia's refusal to export Turkmen gas to hard currency markets and mounting debts of its major customers in the former USSR for gas deliveries contributed to a sharp fall in industrial production and caused the budget to shift from a surplus to a slight deficit. With an authoritarian ex-communist regime in power and a tribally based social structure, Turkmenistan has taken a cautious approach to economic reform, hoping to use gas and cotton sales to sustain its inefficient economy

GDP: *(per capita)*

$5,700

Economic Aid:

$16 million from US

Currency:

Turkmen manat (TMM)

Televisions:

820,000

Transnational Issues:

Limited illicit cultivator of opium poppy, mostly for domestic consumption; limited government eradication programs; increasingly used as transshipment point for illicit drugs from Southwest Asia to Russia and Western Europe; also a transshipment point for acetic anhydride destined for Afghanistan

Turkmenistan Timeline

Late 1800s - Russians conquered and colonized the area which now makes up Turkmenistan
1881 - Turkmen resistance was defeated by Russian forces at the Battle of Geok-Teppe
1920 - The Red Army took control of Ashgabat, securing the entire country
1924 - Turkmen Soviet Socialist Republic was formed
1990 - Turkmenistan declared its sovereignty within the Soviet Union; Saparmurat Niyazov was elected as the first president in October
1991 - Turkmenistan declared its independence in October
1992 - Turkmenistan adopted its constitution in May; Niyazov was reelected as president of the post-Soviet state
2001 - Turkmenistan supported the US Coalition; allowed air corridors for US military aircraft
2002 - Secretary Rumsfield announced continued cooperation between the US and Turkmenistan
2003 - Turkmenistan supported the US/UK attack on Iraq
2004 - General Franks met with Niyazov in Ashbabat to arrange closer US-Turkmen cooperation of military forces
2005 – Turkmen/US continued military/technical information exchange
2007 – Increased US military assistance

United Arab Emirates

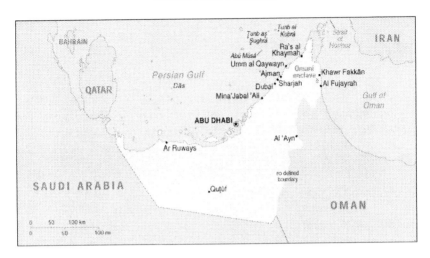

Background:

The Trucial States of the Persian Gulf coast granted the UK control of their defense and foreign affairs in 19th century treaties. In 1971, six of these states – Abu Zaby, 'Ajman, Al Fujayrah, Ash Shariqah, Dubayy, and Umm al Qaywayn – merged to form the UAE. They were joined in 1972 by Ra's al Khaymah. The UAE's per capita GDP is not far below those of the leading West European nations. Its generosity with oil revenues and its moderate foreign policy stance have allowed it to play a vital role in the affairs of the region. The UAE is one of the richest and most important moderate regimes of the Middle East. The UAE allows the presence of US military personnel within its borders

Geography:

Continent: Asia
Total Area: 82,880 sq km, slightly smaller than Maine
Terrain: Flat, barren coastal plain merging into rolling sand dunes of vast desert wasteland, mountains in the east

Climate:

    Desert; cooler in eastern mountains

Environmental Issues:

    Lack of natural freshwater resources being overcome by desalination plants; desertification; beach pollution from oil spills

Population:

    2,563,212 (27% under 15 years of age)

Ethnic Groups:

    Emirati 19%, other Arab and Iranian 23%, South Asian 50%, other expatriates (includes Westerners and East Asians) 8%

Infant Mortality Rate:

    15.58 deaths/1,000 live births

Average Life Expectancy:

    74.75 years

Religions:

    Muslim 96% (Shi'a 16%), Christian, Hindu, and other 4%

Language:

    Arabic (official), Persian, English, Hindi, Urdu

Literacy: *(definition: age 15 and over can read and write)*

    Total Population: 77.9%
    Male: 76.1%
    Female: 81.7%

Government:

>   Federation with specified powers delegated to the UAE federal government and other powers reserved to member emirates

Capital:

>   Abu Dhabi

Economy:

>   The UAE has an open economy with a high per capita income and a sizable annual trade surplus. Its wealth is based on oil and gas output (about 33% of GDP), and the fortunes of the economy fluctuate with the prices of those commodities. Since 1973, the UAE has undergone a profound transformatoin from an impoverished region of small desert principalities to a modern state with a high standard of living. At present levels of production, oil and gas reserves should last for more than 100 years. The UAE has guaranteed President Bush that "cheap" oil will continue to flow no matter how difficult the War on Terrorism becomes

GDP: *(per capita)*

> $25,200

Economic Aid:

>   Donor of 5.2 billion since 1971 to 56 countries

Currency:

>   Emirati dirham (AED)

Televisions:

>   310,000

Military:

> UAE defense policy is based on US protection

Transnational Issues:

> Growing role as heroin trans-shipment and money-laundering center due to its proximity to southwest Asian producing countries and the bustling free trade zone in Dubai

United Arab Emirates Timeline

1853 - "Pirate Coast" sheikdoms signed Treaty of Maritime Peace in perpetuity with UK; truce gave area new name, the "Trucial Coast" or "Trucial Oman"
1892 - Rulers of Trucial Oman signed treaty of protection with UK
1939 - Oil concession granted by Abu Dhabi to Iraq Petroleum Company
1952 - Al Fujayrah became Trucial Oman's seventh sheikdom
1955 - UK, acting on behalf of Abu Dhabi, unilaterally defined sheikdom's boundary with Saudi Arabia
1958 - Discovery of oil in Abu Dhabi; production and export by 1962; OPEC membership by 1967
1966 - Discovery of offshore oil in Dubayy; production by 1970
1968 - UK announced intention to terminate treaty obligations with Arabian Gulf sheikdoms by end of 1971
1971 - Seven Trucial States, together with Bahrain and Qatar, announced provisional formation of the Federation of the Arab Emirates; six sheikdoms formed United Arab Emerites and proclaimed independence; Ras al Khaymah acceded to the union in 1972
1972 - Ruler of Sharjah assassinated in attempted coup; discovery of offshore oil in Sharjah; production by 1974
1974 - Abu Dhabi settled longstanding boundary dispute with Saudi Arabia
1981 - Gulf Cooperation Council (GCC) founded with UAE as charter member
1983 - Discovery of gas-condensate in Ras al Khaymah
1990 - In defiance of Iraqi aggrandizement, the UAE invited US forces to participate in joint air exercises
1990-1991 – The UAE joined coalition forces to oust Iraq from Kuwait
1998 - Abu Dhabi and Dubai began integrating their militaries

2002 - The UAE condemned terrorism; promised stable oil prices throughout the crises; called for redress of Palestinian demands
2003 - The UAE supported Operation Iraqi Freedom
2004 - The UAE offered $1 billion to the Iraq in loans; the UAE continued to support all US military operations related to the reconstruction of Iraq
2006 – Limited support for US efforts in Iraq; increased oil production
2007- Continued UA support for US policy in the Gulf

Uzbekistan

Background:

Russia conquered Uzbekistan in the late 19th century. Stiff resistance to the Red Army after World War I was eventually suppressed and a socialist republic set up in 1925. During the Soviet era, intensive production of "white gold" (cotton) and grain led to overuse of agrochemicals and the depletion of water supplies, which have left the land poisoned and the Aral Sea and certain rivers half dry. Independent since 1991, the country seeks to gradually lessen its dependence on agriculture while developing its mineral and petroleum reserves. Current concerns include insurgency by Islamic militants based in Tajikistan and Afghanistan, a non-convertible currency, and the curtailment of human rights and democratization. Uzbekistan took the boldest action of the former soviet Republics in connection with the war on terrorism. Uzbekistan has become in effect an American ally providing bases for US military action against Al-qaeda and the Taliban

Geography:

Continent: Asia
Total Area: 447,400 sq km, slightly larger than California

Terrain: Mostly flat-to-rolling sandy desert with dunes; broad, flat intensely irrigated river valleys along course of Amu Darya, Sirdayl, and Zarashfson; shrinking Aral Sea in west

Climate:

Mostly midlatitude desert, long, hot summers, mild winters; semiarid grassland in east

Environmental Issues:

Drying up of the Aral Sea is resulting in growing concentrations of chemical pesticides and natural salts; these substances are then blown from the increasingly exposed lake bed and contribute to desertification; water pollution from industrial wastes and the heavy use of fertilizers and pesticides is the cause of many human health disorders; increasing soil Stalinization; soil contamination from agricultural chemicals, including DDT

Population:

26,851,1957 (35% under 15 years of age)

Ethnic Groups:

Uzbek 80%, Russian 5.5%, Tajik, 5%, Karakalpak 2.5%, Tatar 1.5%

Infant Mortality Rate:

71.51 deaths/1,000 live births

Average Life Expectancy:

63.81 years

Religions:

Muslim 88% (mostly Sunnis), Eastern Orthodox 9%, other 3%

Language:

Uzbek 74.3%, Russian 14.2%, Tajik 4.4%, other 7.1%

Literacy: *(definition: age 15 and older can read and write)*

Total population: 99%
Male: 99%
Female: 99%

Government:

Republic; effectively authoritarian presidential rule

Capital:

Tashkent

Economy:

Uzbekistan is a dry, landlocked country of which 10% consists of intensely cultivated, irrigated river valleys. More than 60% of its population lives in densely populated rural communities. Uzbekistan is now the world's third largest cotton exporter, a large producer of gold and oil, and a regionally significant producer of chemicals and machinery. Following independence in December 1991, the government sought to pop up its Soviet-style command economy with subsidies and tight controls on production and prices. Faced with high rates of inflation, however, the government began to reform in mid-1994, by introducing tighter monetary policies, expanding privatization, slightly reducing the role of the state in the economy, and improving the environment for foreign investors. The state continues to be a dominating influence in the economy and has so far failed to bring about much-needed structural changes

GDP: *(per capita)*

$1800

Economic Aid

> Recipient: $276.6 million

Currency:

> Uzbekistani sum (UZS)

Televisions:

> 6.4 million

Transnational Issues:

> Limited illicit cultivation of cannabis and very small amounts of opium poppy, mostly for domestic consumption, almost entirely eradicated by an effective government eradication program; increasingly used as transshipment point for illicit drugs from Afghanistan to Russia and Western Europe and for acetic anhydride destined for Afghanistan

Uzbekistan Timeline

Late 1800s - Russians conquered and colonized the area which now makes up Uzbekistan
1917 - Soviet power was established in Tashkent
1924 - The Uzbekistan region succumbed to the Bolsheviks and became part of the Soviet Union
1990 - Uzbekistan declared sovereignty within the Soviet Union
1991 - Uzbekistan declared independence from the Soviet Union
1992 - The Uzbek Ministry of Defense was formed
2001 - Uzbekistan openly supported the US military; allowed coalition attacks on Afghanistan
2002 - Uzbekistan announced continued military cooperation with the US; increases in US aid promised
2003 - Uzbekistan supported the US/UK attack on Iraq
2004 - US forces used bases in Uzbekistan to fight the war in Afghanistan
2005 - Uzbekistan fully supported Operation Iraqi Freedom; US bases closed in response for US demands for greater Uzbek political reform
2007 – US military aid increased

Terrorist Organizations

Organization	National Affiliation
Abu Sayyaf Group (ASG)	Philippines
Al-Gama'a al-Islamiyya (The Islamic Group, IG)	Egypt
Al-Qa'ida (the Base)	Afghanistan
Armata Corsa	France
Armed Islamic Group (GIA)	Algeria
Aum Shinrikyo	Japan
Basque Homeland and Freedom (ETA)	Spain
Chukaku-Ha (Nucleus or Middle Core Faction)	Japan
Democratic Front for the Liberation of Palestine (DFLP)	Palestinian
Fatah - Revolutionary Council (Abu Nidal Organization)	Lebanon
Fatah Tanzim	Palestinian
Force 17	Palestinian
Hamas (Islamic Resistance Movement)	Palestinian
Harakat ul-Mujahedin (HUM)	Pakistan
Hizballah (Party of God)	Lebanon
Hizb-ul Mujehideen	Pakistan
Irish Republican Army (IRA)	Northern Ireland
Jamaat ul-Fuqra	Pakistan
Japanese Red Army (JRA)	Japan
Jihad Group	Egypt
Kach and Kahane Chai	Israel
Kurdistan Worker's Party (PKK)	Turkey
Lashkar-e-Toiba	Pakistan
Lautaro Youth Movement (MJL)	Chile
Liberation Tigers of Tamil Eelam (LTTE)	Sri Lanka
Loyalist Volunteer Force (LVF)	Northern Ireland
Manuel Rodriquez Patriotic Front (FPMR)	Chile
Moranzanist Patriotic Front (FPM)	Honduras
Mujahedin-e Khalq Organization (MEK or MKO)	Iran
National Liberation Army (ELN) Colombia	Colombia
National Liberation Front of Corsica (FLNC)	France
Nestor Paz Zamora Commission (CNPZ)	Bolivia

New People's Army (NPA)	Philippines
Palestine Liberation Front (PLF)	Iraq
Palestinian Islamic Jihad (PIJ)	Palestinian
Party of Democratic Kampuchea (Khmer Rouge)	Cambodia
Popular Front for the Liberation of Palestine - General Command	Palestinian
Popular Front for the Liberation of Palestine (PFLP)	Palestinian
Popular Struggle Front (PSF)	Syria
Qibla and People Against Gangsterism and Drugs (PAGAD)	South Africa
Real IRA	Northern Ireland
Red Army Faction (RAF)	Germany
Red Brigades (BR)	Italy
Revolutionary Armed Forces of Colombia (FARC)	Colombia
Revolutionary Organization 17 November	Greece
Revolutionary People's Liberation Party/Front (DHCP/F)	Turkey
Revolutionary People's Struggle (ELA)	Greece
Sendero Luminoso (Shining Path)	Peru
Tupac Amaru Revolutionary Movement (MRTA)	Peru

The organization commanding most of the coalition's attention during the first phase of the War on Terrorism was Osama bin Laden's Al Qaeda. Osama bin Laden was probably the most hunted man in the history of the earth. This Saudi expatriate, who was the master architect of the world's most frightening organization, hid in the caves of Afghanistan. He organized and directed his terrorists in perhaps as many as 60 countries. He organized and directed an organization that controlled billions of dollars.

Bin Laden was known to have directed the Sept. 11 attack on the US. He was assumed to have been the dark genius who ordered the bombing of the World Trade Center in New York in 1993 and the Egyptian Embassy in Pakistan two years later. He also arranged the failed attempts to assassinate President George H. W. Bush and President Mubarak of Egypt the same year. Bin Laden no doubt arranged the bloodthirsty assault on the US Embassies in Nairobi and Dar es Salaam in 1998 as well as the attack on the USS Cole in Yemen in 1999. It is impossible to know how many other acts of barbarism may have started within Al-Qaeda.

Osama bin Laden was not the cause of global terrorism nor will his demise end it but Operation Enduring Freedom would not have succeeded until he was eliminated. He was a twisted mix of religious zealot, psychopathic killer, humanitarian, and charismatic leader. His end will mark an important step toward victory in the War on Terrorism. It is commonly argued, probably falsely, that there will always be more bin Ladens to continue the struggle. It is worth noting that the elimination of evil genius, although not a final solution, does often advance the cause of civilization—no one replaced Adolph Hitler, no one replaced Joseph Stalin, and no one replaced the Ayatollah Khomeni.

Once Al Qaeda is eliminated or neutralized, the coalition will turn its attention to other terrorist organizations. The most threatening at the moment are the Hamas and Hizballah which move darkly in and out of Palestine and Lebanon. Both constantly exacerbate the Palestinian-Israeli problem. Both are peculiarly violent and frightening. The elimination of the Iraqi government of Saddam Hussein in 2003 was a massive setback for Hamas and Hizballah. But the death of chairman Arafat in 2004 which might have provided an opening for more moderate Palestinian leaders to return to the Clinton – Barak peace proposals of 1999 lead instead to the takeover of Palestine by Hamas. The establishment of a free and independent Palestine would no doubt substantially reduce the appeal of Hamas and Hizballah. The establishment of free and independent Iraq might be a fatal blow to Muslim fundamentalists. Whether either would be possible was unclear by the end of 2006.

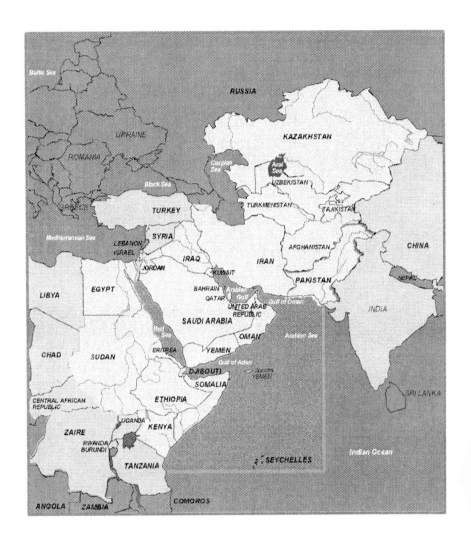

Military Strength Comparisons

Country	Defense Spending($billions)	Military Personnel Active	Military Personnel Reserve	Aircraft	Tanks
USA	$500	1,300,000	1,500,000	18,000	11,600
Supplement Planned	$100				
Great Britain	$50	240,000	260,000	1,857	541
USA and Allies* (Traditional) NATO/Australia, Japan, Korea	$650	5,000,000	10,300,000	34,000	28,000

Note: *Major War Ships: 726 (Including 20 aircraft carriers)

Country	Defense Spending($billions)	Military Personnel Active	Military Personnel Reserve	Aircraft	Tanks
Bahrain	$0.42	11,000	9,850	24	106
Egypt	$2.5	585,000	481,000	585	3,700
Iran	$7.5	545,600	475,000	307	1,390
Iraq	$1.4	429,000	650,000	353	1,900
Israel	$7.0	175,000	430,000	481	4,300
Jordan	$0.5	104,500	30,000	93	1,217
Kuwait	$2.6	15,300	23,700	76	249
Pakistan	$3.3	587,000	513,000	656	2,050
Saudi Arabia	$18.7	162,500	20,000	432	710
Syria	$1.8	423,000	650,000	599	4,600
Turkey	$7.7	624,000	650,000	700	3,500
UAE	$4.5	46,000	0	99	210

Nuclear Weapons Facts--2007

Country	Strategic Warheads	Intermediate/Tactical
USA	8,000*	5,000 (all in the US)
*ICBM = 2000; SLBM = 3000; ALBM = 3000		
Russia	5,000**	8,000 (all in Russia)
**ICBM = 3000; SLBM = 2000; ALBM = 1000		
Great Britain	260	
China	15	400
Israel		100
France	450	
India		60
Pakistan		25
START Projections	2000 within 10 years	0

Note: START involves only the US and Russia

Nations working on nuclear programs: North Korea, Libya, Syria, Iran, Iraq, Algeria.

All strength comparisons and nuclear facts involve classified information—the figures presented here are estimates. The best sources are the US Department of Defense (CDI) an International Institute for Strategic Studies (The Military Balance).

The Academy and the Sea

On June 25, 1997 I started what I knew was going to be a strange, difficult, and exciting journey. The US Navy had asked me to fly to the emirate of Bahrain in the Arabian Gulf and meet the aircraft carrier USS Constellation in order to teach several classes on board the ship. I have always been interested in and fascinated by the Navy and I have always been interested and fascinated by the Gulf—it was easy to agree.

I arrived in Germany on June 26. I only had two days in Germany but I have been there several times before and found once again that I have very strange feelings about Germany. On the bright side, Germany is a remarkably rich, technologically advanced, sophisticated nation. It is astounding to recall that roughly 50 years ago Germany was a defeated nation basically having been leveled and reduced to rubble by the Allies. Now the Federal Republic is the second richest nation on Earth with a robust, industrious population of 90 million people. Also Germany, reunited since 1990 is an extraordinary symbol of the triumph of freedom over the evil empire in 1991. Gone is the Berlin Wall and the Iron Curtain—gone are all the trappings of Soviet madness committed without shame to the enslavement of mankind.

On the not bright side I found myself riding down the Rhine thinking entirely about Germany's horrifying past. To my generation and of course to the earlier generation, I fear Germany will always be a monument to the darkest, most horrible part of human nature. I will never be able to come to grips with how a remarkably educated, refined nation could so enthusiastically have followed the psychopathic rantings of Adolph Hitler— how the people of Bach and Beethoven could have participated in the extermination of six million innocent men, women, and children.

On June 29th I flew to Bahrain which is a once rich, tiny, oil emirate in the middle of the Arabian Gulf. Bahrain means two seas in Arabic indicating that this island nation of 600,000 people is located between the Arabian and Bahrainian Gulfs. Bahrain's population is roughly one half Arab and one half expatriates mostly from South Asia. To make matters very complicated, the Arab population is primarily Shiite while the leadership of the nation is Sunni. It is perfectly obvious that the Emir, who remains an absolute dictator, lives in constant fear of his own population— half having no regard for Arabia as they are in Bahrain solely for the purpose of making money and the majority of the other half are influenced by the sinister forces of Arab fundamentalism. Democratic reform is absolutely out of the question as it would represent nothing short of national suicide.

I had the luxury of visiting Bahrain for one week prior to my work. It is a very modern, rich country with no indication of poverty. The basic social services which present so many fiscal problems for most modern, democratic governments are managed either by the government providing them free of charge or at enormously subsidized prices. Bahrain will soon be out of oil but the emirate has not wasted its natural bounty. It has become, along with the UAE, the banking and the vacation center of the Gulf. All I encountered were fascinated by the United States and its Navy.

My first impression of Bahrain was a stark reminder of the problems of the region and the problems of US foreign policy in the area. I was provided a quite luxurious apartment in the Navy's BOQ (Bachelor Officer's Quarters) called the Manai Plaza. The Manai Plaza is surrounded by marine bunkers manned by some of the toughest looking young Americans I have ever seen. There must have been 200 marines in full battle gear protecting the hotel. They stand 8 hour watches in the most grueling heat known on earth. They appear to not notice the 130 degree temperature and the totally unbearable humidity. The security is really quite unbelievable. My first impression, I am confident, was the same as the view terrorists must have—US marines are trained killers who would have no difficulty carrying out their mission.

On July 3rd I was flown on a C2 to the Constellation which was steaming around the Gulf. Landing on an aircraft carrier, particularly when the pilots are trying to show you the sights, is an experience beyond human calculation. I have always regarded myself as on the fearless side of life, but I was completely terrified. The Carrier appeared to be a little smaller than a postage stamp. The pilots maneuvered the plane to 90 degree angles with the water and then somehow landed on the flight deck. I assumed we had crashed while the pilots commented that it was a great landing. The next day they flew me off the Carrier for a return to Bahrain. The plane I was on hit 140 mph in 2.3 seconds. I do not know exactly know how bullets feel but it must be about the same thing. I discovered planes do not fly off carriers they are shot off carriers. In all, I had four flights on and off the Constellation—my only thought was I shall never go near any plane again. I have dreams now about how wonderful cars and trains are—of course walking is even more perfect. My flight training was completed with a trip on a Black Stallion helicopter. I was sure I had found my natural calling in the sky. I was wrong. Helicopters are just another complicated, terrifying piece of machinery to be avoided by all civilized people.

    By July 5th, I was ready to begin my classes. I had 80 sailors as my students. The officers would come for visits. My four classes started at 0730 and finished at 2200. I taught the same class I teach at the University of San Diego and San Diego State University. I felt my classes went extremely well but of course others will have to judge. What I did find almost beyond belief, was how the students could work 12 hour watches, many on the flight deck in 130 degree temperature wearing long sleeve turtle neck shirts, and arrive in my classes all ready to go. Without exception they showed extraordinary enthusiasm from the first day to the last. To make matters more unusual almost every student was first rate and did an excellent job academically. I told the sailors as I was leaving, my regular students will be forever sorry I visited the USS Constellation because the next time some character appears tired due to a USD or SDSU beer party, I intend to kick them all the way down the hall.

    I was on the Constellation for 36 days, in Bahrain for 10 days, the United Arab Emirates for one week, and had short excursions into four of the smaller Gulf emirates and sultanates. On balance, it was an extraordinary adventure from which I developed several general impressions.

The US Navy

    The Navy like most large organizations wrestles constantly with too much bureaucracy. Bureaucratic problems are compounded by the military tradition of obedience and loyalty. To be a good sailor means to be loyal and obedient even if one is being loyal and obedient to completely bizarre rules and regulations. Because Americans, perhaps more than any other people in the world, are committed to personal freedom, the Navy will always have problems with its bureaucracy.

    The Navy like most organizations is also involved with perhaps 20 percent working harder than anyone can imagine and 80 percent watching. It is particularly fascinating to the outsider because the 20 percent are working in extremely difficult circumstances and all 100 percent may at any time be risking their lives.

    The most interesting aspect of life aboard an American ship of war is how seriously the commitment to the nation is taken. The US Navy has an heroic mission and an heroic past and all in varying ways know it. Sailors would like to be paid a fortune and they would like more benefits and more liberty and all the things all people would like, but they are to a substantial degree motivated by their sense of duty and patriotism. Cynics will never understand the Navy because they cannot fathom this really quite extraordinary state of mind.

One other aspect of Navy life and attitudes which is particularly fascinating from my perspective, is the abiding commitment to the academy. Many enlisted men, they often call themselves squids, joined the Navy because they did not do well in high school, or had no plans for the future, or simply could not afford to go to college. Many in a certain sense regard their civilian past as a failure. In addition, they are dominated by officers who have a marvelous caste system, which is ever mindful of protecting their privileges and position, almost all of whom are university graduates. Thus academic life to the enlisted corps becomes absolutely synonymous with success and with remedying the errors of the past. I chatted with hundreds of squids—they talked constantly about wanting to return to college. They appeared to have no cynicism in their souls—the academy is the avenue to the good life and should be respected in that way.

The Arabs

Beyond the balances of power mentioned above, some general observations about the Gulf Arabs may be useful. The Gulf Arabs are remarkably friendly if suspicious of Western visitors. They are very pro Navy and very pro American. They correctly view the US Navy as their only viable protector and the single force which allows them to escape the tyranny of Saddam or the tyranny of the fundamentalists.

The Shiite-Sunni division in the Gulf is very obvious and important. Bahrain has a population dominated by Shiites which makes it particularly vulnerable but the other Gulf states are primarily Sunni. The entire Gulf is dependent on foreign workers mostly from South Asia who quite obviously have no political loyalty to the Gulf regimes. They in turn have no political rights. The Emirs of the Gulf are feared and respected. There appears to be absolutely no sense of political freedom or political reform in the entire region.

Islam is an overwhelming part of Gulf life. Islam protects the Arabs from Westernization. Islam provides the Arabs with cultural identity and enormous religious satisfaction. The basic tenets of Islam such as prayer five times each day, the idea theirs is the only one God and his only true

prophet is Mohammed, giving substantial alms to the poor, and engaging in a pilgrimage to Mecca are all accepted without question.
The more negative aspects of Islam are equally pervasive. Israel is the enemy and young Gulf Arabs appear to hate the Israelis even more than their fathers did. Women have absolutely no rights in the Western sense and non may be anticipated for the future. America is regarded as both fascinating and a threat in that the American shield one-day may be withdrawn and then all will be lost. The West is a perfect model for economic development and a nightmare for political development. In short, the Gulf specifically and the Middle East generally is the most incredibly anti-democratic place on Earth. All of which compounds the difficulty of America's role and requires enormous American sophistication in order to manage the balances. When one crosses the Red Sea one encounters a magical, strange world without any religious or political freedom and without any desire to change. It is as if 1000 years of history have been missed. Regarding international politics, it is a world without democratic ideology and therefore a world dominated by the often crass clashing of national and religious interests.

Personal Considerations

The downside of my visit to the Gulf and to Constellation is easy to summarize and without much importance. I was terribly homesick—I missed having just a tiny little bit of privacy—the heat was very close to being unbearable—the ship's air conditioning is a creature of the devil designed to make you think it is working but in reality it heats up parts of the ship such as my stateroom—my roommates, two other professors, were charming but crazy---they played chess which I hate and refused to turn on our TV which I love—carriers are huge from the outside but the humans share the ship with 86 planes, there is very little space to do anything expect eat, sleep, and work—the Navy is moving toward a smoke-free system which meant I had to trot up and down eight decks to have a cigarette—warships are incredibly dangerous places, I managed to fall down a ladder one day, broke or dislocated several fingers and was patched up immediately so I would not miss my lecture one hour later—carriers are noisy beyond belief requiring one to wear ear plugs most of the day—and finally we had very little liberty and when we did the Admiral's fear of terrorist attacks meant we had very little freedom while on liberty.
More positively, absolutely every sailor and officer I encountered was polite, courteous, helpful, and always professional. My students were

excellent especially considering the difficulty of the situation. The food was great although I tend to enjoy mediocre food. The ship is a little like a giant country kitchen where quality is made up for by variety. My TV showed all flight operations which was of course fascinating in spite of the fact that the planes were landing about four feet above my bunk. The ship's stores were well stocked and very convenient. Free haircuts and laundry were a treat. Liberty was great fun and the Gulf states are intriguing to visit. Perhaps the highlight of all trips to the region involves shopping for gold in the shouks. The activities of Constellation are extraordinarily interesting. The ship's company is constantly at work carrying out its many missions including sailing the ship, keeping everyone alive, and flying planes. Finally, the flight operations are astounding. Each day the planes took off sometimes more than 50 in a combination of F14s, F18s, C2s, and helicopters. They were flying over Iraq enforcing the no fly zone. They seemed to enjoy scaring the hell out of the Iraqis' on the way to targets and terrifying the Iranians on the way home. My distinct impression was that the Constellation is not only ready but very eager to carry out any orders it might receive. I landed and took off from the carrier several times. My hatred for all planes is now fixed for life.

Conclusion

On August 3rd 1997 I left Constellation. I was taken by a great sense of sadness. Of course I was thrilled to be going home and was hallucinating about swimming in my pool to the end of my days, but I also realized I would probably never again be able to do anything quite so intriguing. The USS Constellation is a great ship serving a great nation. Its officers and crew know something about freedom the rest of us do not— first because they sacrifice so considerably and second, because they serve in such hostile environments. I am positive I shall not live another day without recalling the heroism of the US Navy and recalling what it is they are defending. America is not perfect but at least it is free.

On June 6, 1998 I left San Diego for Norfolk, Va. to join the USS Eisenhower. The Ike was starting its six-month deployment in the Mediterranean, the Adriatic, the Red Sea, and the Gulf. My impressions were almost exactly the same the second time around. We had liberty calls in Spain, France, Italy, and Turkey.

I did, however, have one new experience, which is worth noting. On two different occasions the Ike was ordered to the Adriatic in preparation for an attack against Milosevic's Serbian forces. The attack never came but I was reminded of how tense and frightening battle zone conditions can be. On the lighter side, I was asked if I wanted to leave the ship as combat seemed imminent. I responded I wanted to join an F18 for a bombing run. I had painted my name on a bomb for Milosevic and I wanted to deliver it personally. Somehow I was thought not to be qualified for such a mission.

Dr. Mike Stoddard
December 25, 1998

President George W. Bush

Excerpts: The President's speech November 8, 2001

"Our nation faces a threat to our freedom, and the stakes could not be higher. We are the target of enemies who boast they want to kill—kill all Americans, kill all Jews and kill all Christians. We've seen that type of hate before, and the only possible response is to confront it and to defeat it."

"This enemy tries to hide behind a peaceful faith. But those who celebrate the murder of innocent men, women, and children have no religion, have no conscience and have no mercy."

"We wage a war to save civilization itself."

"Our people have responded with courage and compassion, calm and reason, resolve and fierce determination. We have refused to live in a state of panic or a state of denial. There is a difference between being alert and being intimidated, and this great nation will never be intimidated."

"Too many have the wrong idea of Americans as shallow, materialist consumers who care only about getting rich or getting ahead. But this isn't the America I know."

"We cannot know every turn this battle will take, yet we know our cause is just and ultimate victory is assured. We will no doubt face new challenges, but we have our marching orders. My fellow Americans, let's roll."

Excerpts: The President's State of the Union Address January 29, 2002

"The American flag flies again over our embassy in Kabul. Terrorists who once occupied Afghanistan now occupy cells at Guantanamo Bay. And Terrorist leaders who urged followers to sacrifice their lives are running for their own."

"Our enemies send other people's children on missions of suicide and murder. They embrace tyranny and death as a cause and a creed. We stand for a different choice, made long ago, on the day of our founding. We affirm it again today. We choose freedom and the dignity of every life."

Address to a Joint Session of Congress and the American People
United States Capitol
Washington, D.C.

September 20, 2001

9:00 P.M. EDT

THE PRESIDENT: Mr. Speaker, Mr. President Pro Tempore, members of Congress, and fellow Americans:

In the normal course of events, Presidents come to this chamber to report on the state of the Union. Tonight, no such report is needed. It has already been delivered by the American people.

We have seen it in the courage of passengers, who rushed terrorists to save others on the ground -- passengers like an exceptional man named Todd Beamer. And would you please help me to welcome his wife, Lisa Beamer, here tonight. (Applause.)

We have seen the state of our Union in the endurance of rescuers, working past exhaustion. We have seen the unfurling of flags, the lighting of candles, the giving of blood, the saying of prayers -- in English, Hebrew, and Arabic. We have seen the decency of a loving and giving people who have made the grief of strangers their own.

My fellow citizens, for the last nine days, the entire world has seen for itself the state of our Union -- and it is strong. (Applause.)

Tonight we are a country awakened to danger and called to defend freedom. Our grief has turned to anger, and anger to resolution. Whether we bring our enemies to justice, or bring justice to our enemies, justice will be done. (Applause.)

I thank the Congress for its leadership at such an important time. All of America was touched on the evening of the tragedy to see Republicans and Democrats joined together on the steps of this Capitol, singing "God Bless America." And you did more than sing; you acted, by delivering $40 billion to rebuild our communities and meet the needs of our military.

Speaker Hastert, Minority Leader Gephardt, Majority Leader Daschle and Senator Lott, I thank you for your friendship, for your leadership and for your service to our country. (Applause.)

And on behalf of the American people, I thank the world for its outpouring of support. America will never forget the sounds of our National Anthem playing at Buckingham Palace, on the streets of Paris, and at Berlin's Brandenburg Gate.

We will not forget South Korean children gathering to pray outside our embassy in Seoul, or the prayers of sympathy offered at a mosque in Cairo. We will not forget moments of silence and days of mourning in Australia and Africa and Latin America.

Nor will we forget the citizens of 80 other nations who died with our own: dozens of Pakistanis; more than 130 Israelis; more than 250 citizens of India; men and women from El Salvador, Iran, Mexico and Japan; and hundreds of British citizens. America has no truer friend than Great Britain. (Applause.) Once again, we are joined together in a great cause -- so honored the British Prime Minister has crossed an ocean to show his unity of purpose with America. Thank you for coming, friend. (Applause.)

On September the 11th, enemies of freedom committed an act of war against our country. Americans have known wars -- but for the past 136 years, they have been wars on foreign soil, except for one Sunday in 1941. Americans have known the casualties of war -- but not at the center of a great city on a peaceful morning. Americans have known surprise attacks -- but never before on thousands of civilians. All of this was brought upon us in a single day -- and night fell on a different world, a world where freedom itself is under attack.

Americans have many questions tonight. Americans are asking: Who attacked our country? The evidence we have gathered all points to a collection of loosely affiliated terrorist organizations known as al Qaeda. They are the same murderers indicted for bombing American embassies in Tanzania and Kenya, and responsible for bombing the USS Cole.

Al Qaeda is to terror what the mafia is to crime. But its goal is not making money; its goal is remaking the world -- and imposing its radical beliefs on people everywhere.

The terrorists practice a fringe form of Islamic extremism that has been rejected by Muslim scholars and the vast majority of Muslim clerics -- a fringe movement that perverts the peaceful teachings of Islam. The terrorists' directive commands them to kill Christians and Jews, to kill all Americans, and make no distinction among military and civilians, including women and children.

This group and its leader -- a person named Osama bin Laden -- are linked to many other organizations in different countries, including the Egyptian Islamic Jihad and the Islamic Movement of Uzbekistan. There are thousands of these terrorists in more than 60 countries. They are recruited from their own nations and neighborhoods and brought to camps in places like Afghanistan, where they are trained in the tactics of terror. They are sent back to their homes or sent to hide in countries around the world to plot evil and destruction.

The leadership of al Qaeda has great influence in Afghanistan and supports the Taliban regime in controlling most of that country. In Afghanistan, we see al Qaeda's vision for the world.

Afghanistan's people have been brutalized -- many are starving and many have fled. Women are not allowed to attend school. You can be jailed for owning a television. Religion can be practiced only as their leaders dictate. A man can be jailed in Afghanistan if his beard is not long enough.

The United States respects the people of Afghanistan -- after all, we are currently its largest source of humanitarian aid -- but we condemn the Taliban regime. (Applause.) It is not only repressing its own people, it is threatening people everywhere by sponsoring and sheltering and supplying terrorists. By aiding and abetting murder, the Taliban regime is committing murder.

And tonight, the United States of America makes the following demands on the Taliban: Deliver to United States authorities all the leaders of al Qaeda who hide in your land. (Applause.) Release all foreign nationals, including American citizens, you have unjustly imprisoned. Protect foreign journalists, diplomats and aid workers in your country. Close immediately and permanently every terrorist training camp in Afghanistan, and hand over every terrorist, and every person in their support structure, to appropriate authorities. (Applause.) Give the United States full access to terrorist training camps, so we can make sure they are no longer operating.

These demands are not open to negotiation or discussion. (Applause.) The Taliban must act, and act immediately. They will hand over the terrorists, or they will share in their fate.

I also want to speak tonight directly to Muslims throughout the world. We respect your faith. It's practiced freely by many millions of Americans, and by millions more in countries that America counts as friends. Its teachings are good and peaceful, and those who commit evil in the name of Allah blaspheme the name of Allah. (Applause.) The terrorists are traitors to their own faith, trying, in effect, to hijack Islam itself. The enemy of America is not our many Muslim friends; it is not our many Arab friends. Our enemy is a radical network of terrorists, and every government that supports them. (Applause.)

Our war on terror begins with al Qaeda, but it does not end there. It will not end until every terrorist group of global reach has been found, stopped and defeated. (Applause.)

Americans are asking, why do they hate us? They hate what we see right here in this chamber -- a democratically elected government. Their leaders are self-appointed. They hate our freedoms -- our freedom of religion, our freedom of speech, our freedom to vote and assemble and disagree with each other.

They want to overthrow existing governments in many Muslim countries, such as Egypt, Saudi Arabia, and Jordan. They want to drive Israel out of the Middle East. They want to drive Christians and Jews out of vast regions of Asia and Africa.

These terrorists kill not merely to end lives, but to disrupt and end a way of life. With every atrocity, they hope that America grows fearful, retreating from the world and forsaking our friends. They stand against us, because we stand in their way.

We are not deceived by their pretenses to piety. We have seen their kind before. They are the heirs of all the murderous ideologies of the 20th century. By sacrificing human life to serve their radical visions -- by abandoning every value except the will to power -- they follow in the path of fascism, and Nazism, and totalitarianism. And they will follow that path all the way, to where it ends: in history's unmarked grave of discarded lies. (Applause.)

Americans are asking: How will we fight and win this war? We will direct every resource at our command -- every means of diplomacy, every tool of intelligence, every instrument of law enforcement, every financial influence, and every necessary weapon of war -- to the disruption and to the defeat of the global terror network.

This war will not be like the war against Iraq a decade ago, with a decisive liberation of territory and a swift conclusion. It will not look like the air war above Kosovo two years ago, where no ground troops were used and not a single American was lost in combat.

Our response involves far more than instant retaliation and isolated strikes. Americans should not expect one battle, but a lengthy campaign, unlike any other we have ever seen. It may include dramatic strikes, visible on TV, and covert operations, secret even in success. We will starve terrorists of funding, turn them one against another, drive them from place to place, until there is no refuge or no rest. And we will pursue nations that provide aid or safe haven to terrorism. Every nation, in every region, now has a decision to make. Either you are with us, or you are with the terrorists. (Applause.) From this day forward, any nation that continues to harbor or support terrorism will be regarded by the United States as a hostile regime.

Our nation has been put on notice: We are not immune from attack. We will take defensive measures against terrorism to protect Americans. Today, dozens of federal departments and agencies, as well as state and local governments, have responsibilities affecting homeland security. These efforts must be coordinated at the highest level. So tonight I announce the creation of a Cabinet-level position reporting directly to me -- the Office of Homeland Security.

And tonight I also announce a distinguished American to lead this effort, to strengthen American security: a military veteran, an effective governor, a true patriot, a trusted friend -- Pennsylvania's Tom Ridge. (Applause.) He will lead, oversee and coordinate a comprehensive national strategy to safeguard our country against terrorism, and respond to any attacks that may come.

These measures are essential. But the only way to defeat terrorism as a threat to our way of life is to stop it, eliminate it, and destroy it where it grows. (Applause.)

Many will be involved in this effort, from FBI agents to intelligence operatives to the reservists we have called to active duty. All deserve our thanks, and all have our prayers. And tonight, a few miles from the damaged Pentagon, I have a message for our military: Be ready. I've called the Armed Forces to alert, and there is a reason. The hour is coming when America will act, and you will make us proud. (Applause.)

This is not, however, just America's fight. And what is at stake is not just America's freedom. This is the world's fight. This is civilization's fight. This is the fight of all who believe in progress and pluralism, tolerance and freedom.

We ask every nation to join us. We will ask, and we will need, the help of police forces, intelligence services, and banking systems around the world. The United States is grateful that many nations and many international organizations have already responded -- with sympathy and with support. Nations from Latin America, to Asia, to Africa, to Europe, to the Islamic world. Perhaps the NATO Charter reflects best the attitude of the world: An attack on one is an attack on all.

The civilized world is rallying to America's side. They understand that if this terror goes unpunished, their own cities, their own citizens may be next. Terror, unanswered, can not only bring down buildings, it can threaten the stability of legitimate governments. And you know what -- we're not going to allow it. (Applause.)

Americans are asking: What is expected of us? I ask you to live your lives, and hug your children. I know many citizens have fears tonight, and I ask you to be calm and resolute, even in the face of a continuing threat.

I ask you to uphold the values of America, and remember why so many have come here. We are in a fight for our principles, and our first responsibility is to live by them. No one should be singled out for unfair treatment or unkind words because of their ethnic background or religious faith. (Applause.)

I ask you to continue to support the victims of this tragedy with your contributions. Those who want to give can go to a central source of information, libertyunites.org, to find the names of groups providing direct help in New York, Pennsylvania, and Virginia.

The thousands of FBI agents who are now at work in this investigation may need your cooperation, and I ask you to give it.

I ask for your patience, with the delays and inconveniences that may accompany tighter security; and for your patience in what will be a long struggle.

I ask your continued participation and confidence in the American economy. Terrorists attacked a symbol of American prosperity. They did not touch its source. America is successful because of the hard work, and creativity, and enterprise of our people. These were the true strengths of our economy before September 11th, and they are our strengths today. (Applause.)

And, finally, please continue praying for the victims of terror and their families, for those in uniform, and for our great country. Prayer has comforted us in sorrow, and will help strengthen us for the journey ahead.

Tonight I thank my fellow Americans for what you have already done and for what you will do. And ladies and gentlemen of the Congress, I thank you, their representatives, for what you have already done and for what we will do together.

Tonight, we face new and sudden national challenges. We will come together to improve air safety, to dramatically expand the number of air marshals on domestic flights, and take new measures to prevent hijacking. We will come together to promote stability and keep our airlines flying, with direct assistance during this emergency. (Applause.)

We will come together to give law enforcement the additional tools it needs to track down terror here at home. (Applause.) We will come together to strengthen our intelligence capabilities to know the plans of terrorists before they act, and find them before they strike. (Applause.)

We will come together to take active steps that strengthen America's economy, and put our people back to work.

Tonight we welcome two leaders who embody the extraordinary spirit of all New Yorkers: Governor George Pataki, and Mayor Rudolph Giuliani. (Applause.) As a symbol of America's resolve, my administration will work with Congress, and these two leaders, to show the world that we will rebuild New York City. (Applause.)

After all that has just passed -- all the lives taken, and all the possibilities and hopes that died with them -- it is natural to wonder if America's future is one of fear. Some speak of an age of terror. I know there are struggles ahead, and dangers to face. But this country will define our times, not be defined by them. As long as the United States of America is determined and strong, this will not be an age of terror; this will be an age of liberty, here and across the world. (Applause.)

Great harm has been done to us. We have suffered great loss. And in our grief and anger we have found our mission and our moment. Freedom and fear are at war. The advance of human freedom -- the great achievement of our time, and the great hope of every time -- now depends on us. Our nation -- this generation -- will lift a dark threat of violence from our people and our future. We will rally the world to this cause by our efforts, by our courage. We will not tire, we will not falter, and we will not fail. (Applause.)

It is my hope that in the months and years ahead, life will return almost to normal. We'll go back to our lives and routines, and that is good. Even grief recedes with time and grace. But our resolve must not pass. Each of us will remember what happened that day, and to whom it happened. We'll remember the moment the news came -- where we were and what we were doing. Some will remember an image of a fire, or a story of rescue. Some will carry memories of a face and a voice gone forever.

And I will carry this: It is the police shield of a man named George Howard, who died at the World Trade Center trying to save others. It was given to me by his mom, Arlene, as a proud memorial to her son. This is my reminder of lives that ended, and a task that does not end. (Applause.)

I will not forget this wound to our country or those who inflicted it. I will not yield; I will not rest; I will not relent in waging this struggle for freedom and security for the American people.

The course of this conflict is not known, yet its outcome is certain. Freedom and fear, justice and cruelty, have always been at war, and we know that God is not neutral between them. (Applause.)

Fellow citizens, we'll meet violence with patient justice -- assured of the rightness of our cause, and confident of the victories to come. In all that lies before us, may God grant us wisdom, and may He watch over the United States of America. Thank you.

Presidential Address -- USS Abraham Lincoln

May 1, 2003

THE PRESIDENT: Admiral Kelly, Captain Card, officers and sailors of the USS Abraham Lincoln, and my fellow Americans: Major combat operations in Iraq have ended. In the Battle of Iraq, the United States and our allies have prevailed. And now our coalition is engaged in securing and reconstructing that country.

In this battle, we have fought for the cause of liberty, and for the peace of the world. Our Nation and our coalition are proud of this accomplishment yet it is you, the members of the United States military, who achieved it. Your courage -- your willingness to face danger for your country and for each other --made this day possible. Because of you, our Nation is more secure. Because of you, the tyrant has fallen, and Iraq is free.

Operation Iraqi Freedom was carried out with a combination of precision, speed, and boldness the enemy did not expect, and the world had not seen before. From distant bases or ships at sea, we sent planes and missiles that could destroy an enemy division, or strike a single bunker. Marines and soldiers charged to Baghdad across 350 miles of hostile ground, in one of the swiftest advances of heavy arms in history. You have shown the world the skill and might of the American Armed Forces.

This Nation thanks all the members of our coalition who joined in a noble cause. We thank the Armed Forces of the United Kingdom, Australia, and Poland, who shared in the hardships of war. We thank all the citizens of Iraq who welcomed our troops and joined in the liberation of their own country. And tonight, I have a special word for Secretary Rumsfeld, for General Franks, andfor all the men and women who wear the uniform of the United States: America is grateful for a job well done.

The character of our military through history -- the daring of Normandy, the fierce courage of Iwo Jima, the decency and idealism that turned enemies into allies -- is fully present in this generation. When Iraqi civilians looked into the faces of our servicemen and women, they saw strength, and kindness, and goodwill. When I look at the members of the United States military, I see the best of our country, and I am honored to be your Commander in Chief.

In the images of falling statues, we have witnessed the arrival of a new era.

For a hundred years of war, culminating in the nuclear age, military technology was designed and deployed to inflict casualties on an ever-growing scale. In defeating Nazi Germany and imperial Japan, Allied Forces destroyed entire cities, while enemy leaders who started the conflict were safe until the final days. Military power was used to end a regime by breaking a nation. Today, we have the greater power to free a nation by breaking a dangerous and aggressive regime. With new tactics and precision weapons, we can achieve military objectives without directing violence against civilians. No device of man can remove the tragedy from war. Yet it is a great advance when the guilty have far more to fear from war than the innocent.

In the images of celebrating Iraqis, we have also seen the ageless appeal of human freedom. Decades of lies and intimidation could not make the Iraqi people love their oppressors or desire their own enslavement. Men and women in every culture need liberty like they need food, and water, and air. Everywhere that freedom arrives, humanity rejoices. And everywhere that freedom stirs, let tyrants fear.

We have difficult work to do in Iraq. We are bringing order to parts of that country that remain dangerous. We are pursuing and finding leaders of the old regime, who will be held to account for their crimes. We have begun the search for hidden chemical and biological weapons, and already know of hundreds of sites that will be investigated. We are helping to rebuild Iraq, where the dictator built palaces for himself, instead of hospitals and schools for the people. And we will stand with the new leaders of Iraq as they establish a government of, by, and for the Iraqi people. The transition from dictatorship to democracy will take time, but it is worth every effort. Our coalition will stay until our work is done. Then we will leave -- and we will leave behind a free Iraq.

The Battle of Iraq is one victory in a war on terror that began on September 11th, 2001, and still goes on. That terrible morning, 19 evil men -- the shock troops of a hateful ideology -- gave America and the civilized world a glimpse of their ambitions. They imagined, in the words of one terrorist, that September 11th would be the "beginning of the end of America." By seeking to turn our cities into killing fields, terrorists and their allies believed they could destroy this Nation's resolve, and force our retreat from the world. They have failed.

In the Battle of Afghanistan, we destroyed the Taliban, many terrorists, and the camps where they trained. We continue to help the Afghan people lay roads, restore hospitals, and educate all of their children. Yet we also have dangerous work to complete. And as I speak, a special operations task force, led by the 82nd Airborne, is on the trail of terrorists, and those who seek to undermine the free government of Afghanistan. America and our coalition will finish what we began.

From Pakistan to the Philippines to the Horn of Africa, we are hunting down al-Qaida killers. Nineteen months ago, I pledged that the terrorists would not escape the patient justice of the United States. As of tonight, nearly one-half of al-Qaida's senior operatives have been captured or killed.

The liberation of Iraq is a crucial advance in the campaign against terror. We have removed an ally of al-Qaida, and cut off a source of terrorist funding. And this much is certain: No terrorist network will gain weapons of mass destruction from the Iraqi regime, because that regime is no more.

In these 19 months that changed the world, our actions have been focused, and deliberate, and proportionate to the offense. We have not forgotten the victims of September 11th -- the last phone calls, the cold murder of children, the searches in the rubble. With those attacks, the terrorists and their supporters declared war on the United States. And war is what they got.

Our war against terror is proceeding according to principles that I have made clear to all:

Any person involved in committing or planning terrorist attacks against the American people becomes an enemy of this country, and a target of American justice.

Any person, organization, or government that supports, protects, or harbors terrorists is complicit in the murder of the innocent, and equally guilty of terrorist crimes.

Any outlaw regime that has ties to terrorist groups, and seeks or possesses weapons of mass destruction, is a grave danger to the civilized world, and will be confronted.

And anyone in the world, including the Arab world, who works and sacrifices for freedom has a loyal friend in the United States.

Our commitment to liberty is America's tradition -- declared at our founding

-- affirmed in Franklin Roosevelt's Four Freedoms -- asserted in the Truman Doctrine, and in Ronald Reagan's challenge to an evil empire. We are committed to freedom in Afghanistan, in Iraq, and in a peaceful Palestine. The advance of freedom is the surest strategy to undermine the appeal of terror in the world. Where freedom takes hold, hatred gives way to hope. When freedom takes hold, men and women turn to the peaceful pursuit of a better life. American values, and American interests, lead in the same direction: We stand for human liberty.

The United States upholds these principles of security and freedom in many ways -- with all the tools of diplomacy, law enforcement, intelligence, and finance. We are working with a broad coalition of nations that understand the threat, and our shared responsibility to meet it. The use of force has been, and remains, our last resort. Yet all can know, friend and foe alike, that our Nation has a mission: We will answer threats to our security, and we will defend the peace.

Our mission continues. Al-Qaida is wounded, not destroyed. The scattered cells of the terrorist network still operate in many nations, and we know from daily intelligence that they continue to plot against free people. The proliferation of deadly weapons remains a serious danger. The enemies of freedom are not idle, and neither are we. Our government has taken unprecedented measures to defend the homeland -- and we will continue to hunt down the enemy before he can strike.

The war on terror is not over, yet it is not endless. We do not know the day of final victory, but we have seen the turning of the tide. No act of the terrorists will change our purpose, or weaken our resolve, or alter their fate. Their cause is lost. Free nations will press on to victory.

Other nations in history have fought in foreign lands and remained to occupy and exploit. Americans, following a battle, want nothing more than to return home. That is your direction tonight. After service in the Afghan and Iraqi theatres of war -- after 100 thousand miles, on the longest carrier deployment in recent history -- you are homeward bound. Some of you will see new family members for the first time -- 150 babies were born while their fathers were on the Lincoln. Your families are proud of you, and your Nation will welcome you.

We are mindful as well that some good men and women are not making the journey home. One of those who fell, Corporal Jason Mileo, spoke to his parents five days before his death. Jason's father said, "He called us from the center of Baghdad, not to brag, but to tell us he loved us. Our son was a soldier." Every name, every life, is a loss to our military, to our Nation, and to loved ones who grieve. There is no homecoming for these families. Yet we pray, in God's time, their reunion will come.

Those we lost were last seen on duty. Their final act on this earth was to fight a great evil, and bring liberty to others. All of you -- all in this generation of our military -- have taken up the highest calling of history. You are defending your country, and protecting the innocent from harm. And wherever you go, you carry a message of hope -- a message that is ancient, and ever new. In the words of the prophet Isaiah: "To the captives, 'Come out,' -- and to those in darkness, 'Be free.'"

Thank you for serving our country and our cause. God bless you all, and may God bless America.

Prime Minister Blair's Address to Congress

Thursday, July 17, 2003 Posted: 9:44 PM EDT (0144 GMT)

WASHINGTON (CNN) -- Britain's Prime Minister Tony Blair addressed a joint session of the U.S. Congress on Thursday, July 17, 2003. Here is a transcript of his speech.

Mr. Speaker and Mr. Vice President, honorable members of Congress, I'm deeply touched by that warm and generous welcome. That's more than I deserve and more than I'm used to, quite frankly.

And let me begin by thanking you most sincerely for voting to award me the Congressional Gold Medal. But you, like me, know who the real heroes are: those brave service men and women, yours and ours, who fought the war and risk their lives still.

And our tribute to them should be measured in this way, by showing them and their families that they did not strive or die in vain, but that through their sacrifice future generations can live in greater peace, prosperity and hope.

Let me also express my gratitude to President Bush. Through the troubled times since September the 11th changed our world, we have been allies and friends. Thank you, Mr. President, for your leadership.

Mr. Speaker, sir, my thrill on receiving this award was only a little diminished on being told that the first Congressional Gold Medal was awarded to George Washington for what Congress called his "wise and spirited conduct" in getting rid of the British out of Boston.

On our way down here, Senator Frist was kind enough to show me the fireplace where, in 1814, the British had burnt the Congress Library. I know this is, kind of, late, but sorry.

Actually, you know, my middle son was studying 18th century history and the American War of Independence, and he said to me the other day, "You know, Lord North, Dad, he was the British prime minister who lost us America. So just think, however many mistakes you'll make, you'll never make one that bad."

Members of Congress, I feel a most urgent sense of mission about today's world.

September 11 was not an isolated event, but a tragic prologue, Iraq another act, and many further struggles will be set upon this stage before it's over.

There never has been a time when the power of America was so necessary or so misunderstood, or when, except in the most general sense, a study of history provides so little instruction for our present day.

We were all reared on battles between great warriors, between great nations, between powerful forces and ideologies that dominated entire continents. And these were struggles for conquest, for land, or money, and the wars were fought by massed armies. And the leaders were openly acknowledged, the outcomes decisive.

Today, none of us expect our soldiers to fight a war on our own territory. The immediate threat is not conflict between the world's most powerful nations.

And why? Because we all have too much to lose. Because technology, communication, trade and travel are bringing us ever closer together. Because in the last 50 years, countries like yours and mine have tripled their growth and standard of living. Because even those powers like Russia or China or India can see the horizon, the future wealth, clearly and know they are on a steady road toward it. And because all nations that are free value that freedom, will defend it absolutely, but have no wish to trample on the freedom of others.

We are bound together as never before. And this coming together provides us with unprecedented opportunity but also makes us uniquely vulnerable.

And the threat comes because in another part of our globe there is shadow and darkness, where not all the world is free, where many millions suffer under brutal dictatorship, where a third of our planet lives in a poverty beyond anything even the poorest in our societies can imagine, and where a fanatical strain of religious extremism has arisen, that is a mutation of the true and peaceful faith of Islam.

And because in the combination of these afflictions a new and deadly virus has emerged. The virus is terrorism whose intent to inflict destruction is unconstrained by human feeling and whose capacity to inflict it is enlarged by technology.

This is a battle that can't be fought or won only by armies. We are so much more powerful in all conventional ways than the terrorists, yet even in all our might, we are taught humility.

In the end, it is not our power alone that will defeat this evil. Our ultimate weapon is not our guns, but our beliefs.

There is a myth that though we love freedom, others don't; that our attachment to freedom is a product of our culture; that freedom, democracy, human rights, the rule of law are American values, or Western values; that Afghan women were content under the lash of the Taliban; that Saddam was somehow beloved by his people; that Milosevic was Serbia's savior.

Members of Congress, ours are not Western values, they are the universal values of the human spirit. And anywhere...

Anywhere, anytime ordinary people are given the chance to choose, the choice is the same: freedom, not tyranny; democracy, not dictatorship; the rule of law, not the rule of the secret police.

The spread of freedom is the best security for the free. It is our last line of defense and our first line of attack. And just as the terrorist seeks to divide humanity in hate, so we have to unify it around an idea. And that idea is liberty.

We must find the strength to fight for this idea and the compassion to make it universal.

Abraham Lincoln said, "Those that deny freedom to others deserve it not for themselves."

And it is this sense of justice that makes moral the love of liberty.

In some cases where our security is under direct threat, we will have recourse to arms. In others, it will be by force of reason. But in all cases, to the same end: that the liberty we seek is not for some but for all, for that is the only true path to victory in this struggle.

But first we must explain the danger.

Our new world rests on order. The danger is disorder. And in today's world, it can now spread like contagion.

The terrorists and the states that support them don't have large armies or precision weapons; they don't need them. Their weapon is chaos.

The purpose of terrorism is not the single act of wanton destruction. It is the reaction it seeks to provoke: economic collapse, the backlash, the hatred, the division, the elimination of tolerance, until societies cease to reconcile their differences and become defined by them. Kashmir, the Middle East, Chechnya, Indonesia, Africa--barely a continent or nation is unscathed.

The risk is that terrorism and states developing weapons of mass destruction come together. And when people say, "That risk is fanciful," I say we know the Taliban supported Al Qaida. We know Iraq under Saddam gave haven to and supported terrorists. We know there are states in the Middle East now actively funding and helping people, who regard it as God's will in the act of suicide to take as many innocent lives with them on their way to God's judgment.

Some of these states are desperately trying to acquire nuclear weapons. We know that companies and individuals with expertise sell it to the highest bidder, and we know that at least one state, North Korea, lets its people starve while spending billions of dollars on developing nuclear weapons and exporting the technology abroad.

This isn't fantasy, it is 21st-century reality, and it confronts us now.

Can we be sure that terrorism and weapons of mass destruction will join together? Let us say one thing: If we are wrong, we will have destroyed a threat that at its least is responsible for inhuman carnage and suffering. That is something I am confident history will forgive.

But if our critics are wrong, if we are right, as I believe with every fiber of instinct and conviction I have that we are, and we do not act, then we will have hesitated in the face of this menace when we should have given leadership. That is something history will not forgive.

But precisely because the threat is new, it isn't obvious. It turns upside-down our concepts of how we should act and when, and it crosses the frontiers of many nations. So just as it redefines our notions of security, so it must refine our notions of diplomacy.

There is no more dangerous theory in international politics than that we need to balance the power of America with other competitive powers; different poles around which nations gather.

Such a theory may have made sense in 19th-century Europe. It was perforce the position in the Cold War.

Today, it is an anachronism to be discarded like traditional theories of security. And it is dangerous because it is not rivalry but partnership we need; a common will and a shared purpose in the face of a common threat.

And I believe any alliance must start with America and Europe. If Europe and America are together, the others will work with us. If we split, the rest will play around, play us off and nothing but mischief will be the result of it.

You may think after recent disagreements it can't be done, but the debate in Europe is open. Iraq showed that when, never forget, many European nations supported our action.

And it shows it still when those that didn't agreed Resolution 1483 in the United Nations for Iraq's reconstruction.

Today, German soldiers lead in Afghanistan, French soldiers lead in the Congo where they stand between peace and a return to genocide.

So we should not minimize the differences, but we should not let them confound us either.

You know, people ask me after the past months when, let's say, things were a trifle strained in Europe, "Why do you persist in wanting Britain at the center of Europe?" And I say, "Well, maybe if the U.K. were a group of islands 20 miles off Manhattan, I might feel differently. But actually, we're 20 miles off Calais and joined by a tunnel."

We are part of Europe, and we want to be. But we also want to be part of changing Europe.

Europe has one potential for weakness. For reasons that are obvious, we spent roughly a thousand years killing each other in large numbers.

The political culture of Europe is inevitably rightly based on compromise. Compromise is a fine thing except when based on an illusion. And I don't believe you can compromise with this new form of terrorism.

But Europe has a strength. It is a formidable political achievement. Think of the past and think of the unity today. Think of it preparing to reach out even to Turkey--a nation of vastly different culture, tradition, religion--and welcome it in.

But my real point is this: Now Europe is at the point of transformation. Next year, 10 new countries will join. Romania and Bulgaria will follow.

Why will these new European members transform Europe? Because their scars are recent, their memories strong, their relationship with freedom still one of passion, not comfortable familiarity.

They believe in the trans-Atlantic alliance. They support economic reform. They want a Europe of nations, not a super state. They are our allies and they are yours. So don't give up on Europe. Work with it.

To be a serious partner, Europe must take on and defeat the anti-Americanism that sometimes passes for its political discourse. And what America must do is show that this is a partnership built on persuasion, not command.

Then the other great nations of our world and the small will gather around in one place, not many. And our understanding of this threat will become theirs. And the United Nations can then become what it should be: an instrument of action as well as debate.

The Security Council should be reformed. We need a new international regime on the nonproliferation of weapons of mass destruction.

And we need to say clearly to United Nations members: "If you engage in the systematic the mission the coalition. But let us start preferring a coalition and acting alone if we have to, not the other way around.

True, winning wars is not easier that way, but winning the peace is.

And we have to win both. And you have an extraordinary record of doing so.

Who helped Japan renew, or Germany reconstruct, or Europe get back on its feet after World War II? America.

So when we invade Afghanistan or Iraq, our responsibility does not end with military victory.

Finishing the fighting is not finishing the job.

So if Afghanistan needs more troops from the international community to police outside Kabul, our duty is to get them.

Let us help them eradicate their dependency on the poppy, the crop whose wicked residue turns up on the streets of Britain as heroin to destroy young British lives, as much as their harvest warps the lives of Afghans.

We promised Iraq democratic government. We will deliver it.

We promised them the chance to use their oil wealth to build prosperity for all their citizens, not a corrupt elite, and we will do so. We will stay with these people so in need of our help until the job is done.

And then reflect on this: How hollow would the charges of American imperialism be when these failed countries are and are seen to be transformed from states of terror to nations of prosperity, from governments of dictatorship to examples of democracy, from sources of instability to beacons of calm.

And how risible would be the claims that these were wars on Muslims if the world could see these Muslim nations still Muslim, but with some hope for the future, not shackled by brutal regimes whose principal victims were the very Muslims they pretended to protect?

It would be the most richly observed advertisement for the values of freedom we can imagine. When we removed the Taliban and Saddam Hussein, this was not imperialism. For these oppressed people, it was their liberation.

And why can the terrorists even mount an argument in the Muslim world that it isn't?

Because there is one cause terrorism rides upon, a cause they have no belief in but can manipulate. I want to be very plain: This terrorism will not be defeated without peace in the Middle East between Israel and Palestine.

Here it is that the poison is incubated. Here it is that the extremist is able to confuse in the mind of a frighteningly large number of people the case for a Palestinian state and the destruction of Israel, and to translate this moreover into a battle between East and West, Muslim, Jew and Christian.

May this never compromise the security of the state of Israel.

The state of Israel should be recognized by the entire Arab world, and the vile propaganda used to indoctrinate children, not just against Israel but against Jews, must cease.

You cannot teach people hate and then ask them to practice peace. But neither can you teach people peace except by according them dignity and granting them hope.

Innocent Israelis suffer. So do innocent Palestinians.

The ending of Saddam's regime in Iraq must be the starting point of a new dispensation for the Middle East: Iraq, free and stable; Iran and Syria, who give succor to the rejectionist men of violence, made to realize that the world will no longer countenance it, that the hand of friendship can only be offered them if they resile completely from this malice, but that if they do, that hand will be there for them and their people; the whole of region helped toward democracy. And to symbolize it all, the creation of an independent, viable and democratic Palestinian state side by side with the state of Israel.

What the president is doing in the Middle East is tough but right.

And let me at this point thank the president for his support, and that of President Clinton before him, and the support of members of this Congress, for our attempts to bring peace to Northern Ireland.

You know, one thing I've learned about peace processes: They're always frustrating, they're often agonizing, and occasionally they seem hopeless. But for all that, having a peace process is better than not having one.

And why has a resolution of Palestine such a powerful appeal across the world? Because it embodies an even-handed approach to justice, just as when this president recommended and this Congress supported a $15 billion increase in spending on the world's poorest nations to combat HIV/AIDS. It was a statement of concern that echoed rightly around the world.

There can be no freedom for Africa without justice and no justice without declaring war on Africa's poverty, disease and famine with as much vehemence as we removed the tyrant and the terrorists.

In Mexico in September, the world should unite and give us a trade round that opens up our markets. I'm for free trade, and I'll tell you why: because we can't say to the poorest people in the world, "We want you to be free, but just don't try to sell your goods in our market."

And because ever since the world started to open up, it has prospered. And that prosperity has to be environmentally sustainable, too.

You know, I remember at one of our earliest international meetings, a European prime minister telling President Bush that the solution was quite simple: Just double the tax on American gasoline.

Your president gave him a most eloquent look.

It reminded me of the first leader of my party, Keir Hardy, in the early part of the 20th century.

He was a man who used to correspond with the Pankhursts, the great campaigners for women's votes.

And shortly before the election, June 1913, one of the Pankhursts sisters wrote to Hardy saying she had been studying Britain carefully and there was a worrying rise in sexual immorality linked to heavy drinking. So she suggested he fight the election on the platform of votes for women, chastity for men and prohibition for all.

He replied saying, "Thank you for your advice. The electoral benefits of which are not immediately discernible."

We all get that kind of advice, don't we?

But frankly, we need to go beyond even Kyoto, and science and technology is the way.

Climate change, deforestation, the voracious drain on natural resources cannot be ignored. Unchecked, these forces will hinder the economic development of the most vulnerable nations first and ultimately all nations.

So we must show the world that we are willing to step up to these challenges around the world and in our own backyards.

Members of Congress, if this seems a long way from the threat of terror and weapons of mass destruction, it is only to say again that the world security cannot be protected without the world's heart being one. So America must listen as well as lead. But, members of Congress, don't ever apologize for your values.

Tell the world why you're proud of America. Tell them when the Star-Spangled Banner starts, Americans get to their feet, Hispanics, Irish, Italians, Central Europeans, East Europeans, Jews, Muslims, white, Asian, black, those who go back to the early settlers and those whose English is the same as some New York cab driver's I've dealt with ... but whose sons and daughters could run for this Congress.

Tell them why Americans, one and all, stand upright and respectful. Not because some state official told them to, but because whatever race, color, class or creed they are, being American means being free. That's why they're proud.

As Britain knows, all predominant power seems for a time invincible, but, in fact, it is transient.

The question is: What do you leave behind?

And what you can bequeath to this anxious world is the light of liberty.

That is what this struggle against terrorist groups or states is about. We're not fighting for domination. We're not fighting for an American world, though we want a world in which America is at ease. We're not fighting for Christianity, but against religious fanaticism of all kinds.

And this is not a war of civilizations, because each civilization has a unique capacity to enrich the stock of human heritage.

We are fighting for the inalienable right of humankind--black or white, Christian or not, left, right or a million different--to be free, free to raise a family in love and hope, free to earn a living and be rewarded by your efforts, free not to bend your knee to any man in fear, free to be you so long as being you does not impair the freedom of others.

That's what we're fighting for. And it's a battle worth fighting.

And I know it's hard on America, and in some small corner of this vast country, out in Nevada or Idaho or these places I've never been to, but always wanted to go...

I know out there there's a guy getting on with his life, perfectly happily, minding his own business, saying to you, the political leaders of this country, "Why me? And why us? And why America?"

And the only answer is, "Because destiny put you in this place in history, in this moment in time, and the task is yours to do."

And our job, my nation that watched you grow, that you fought alongside and now fights alongside you, that takes enormous pride in our alliance and great affection in our common bond, our job is to be there with you.

You are not going to be alone. We will be with you in this fight for liberty.

We will be with you in this fight for liberty. And if our spirit is right and our courage firm, the world will be with us.

Thank you.

President Bush Discusses Freedom in Iraq and Middle East

Remarks by the President at the 20th Anniversary of the National Endowment for Democracy
United States Chamber of Commerce
Washington, D.C.
11:05 A.M. EST

THE PRESIDENT: Thank you all very much. Please be seated. Thanks for the warm welcome, and thanks for inviting me to join you in this 20th anniversary of the National Endowment for Democracy. The staff and directors of this organization have seen a lot of history over the last two decades, you've been a part of that history. By speaking for and standing for freedom, you've lifted the hopes of people around the world, and you've brought great credit to America.

I appreciate Vin for the short introduction. I'm a man who likes short introductions. And he didn't let me down. But more importantly, I appreciate the invitation. I appreciate the members of Congress who are here, senators from both political parties, members of the House of Representatives from both political parties. I appreciate the ambassadors who are here. I appreciate the guests who have come. I appreciate the bipartisan spirit, the nonpartisan spirit of the National Endowment for Democracy. I'm glad that Republicans and Democrats and independents are working together to advance human liberty.

The roots of our democracy can be traced to England, and to its Parliament -- and so can the roots of this organization. In June of 1982, President Ronald Reagan spoke at Westminster Palace and declared, the turning point had arrived in history. He argued that Soviet communism had failed, precisely because it did not respect its own people -- their creativity, their genius and their rights.

President Reagan said that the day of Soviet tyranny was passing, that freedom had a momentum which would not be halted. He gave this organization its mandate: to add to the momentum of freedom across the world. Your mandate was important 20 years ago; it is equally important today. (Applause.)

A number of critics were dismissive of that speech by the President. According to one editorial of the time, "It seems hard to be a sophisticated European and also an admirer of Ronald Reagan." (Laughter.) Some observers on both sides of the Atlantic pronounced the speech simplistic and naive, and even dangerous. In fact, Ronald Reagan's words were courageous and optimistic and entirely correct. (Applause.)

The great democratic movement President Reagan described was already well underway. In the early 1970s, there were about 40 democracies in the world. By the middle of that decade, Portugal and Spain and Greece held free elections. Soon there were new democracies in Latin America, and free institutions were spreading in Korea, in Taiwan, and in East Asia. This very week in 1989, there were protests in East Berlin and in Leipzig. By the end of that year, every communist dictatorship in Central America* had collapsed. Within another year, the South African government released Nelson Mandela. Four years later, he was elected president of his country -- ascending, like Walesa and Havel, from prisoner of state to head of state.

As the 20th century ended, there were around 120 democracies in the world -- and I can assure you more are on the way. (Applause.) Ronald Reagan would be pleased, and he would not be surprised.

We've witnessed, in little over a generation, the swiftest advance of freedom in the 2,500 year story of democracy. Historians in the future will offer their own explanations for why this happened. Yet we already know some of the reasons they will cite. It is no accident that the rise of so many democracies took place in a time when the world's most influential nation was itself a democracy.

The United States made military and moral commitments in Europe and Asia, which protected free nations from aggression, and created the conditions in which new democracies could flourish. As we provided security for whole nations, we also provided inspiration for oppressed peoples. In prison camps, in banned union meetings, in clandestine churches, men and women knew that the whole world was not sharing their own nightmare. They knew of at least one place -- a bright and hopeful land -- where freedom was valued and secure. And they prayed that America would not forget them, or forget the mission to promote liberty around the world.

Historians will note that in many nations, the advance of markets and free enterprise helped to create a middle class that was confident enough to demand their own rights. They will point to the role of technology in frustrating censorship and central control -- and marvel at the power of instant communications to spread the truth, the news, and courage across borders.

Historians in the future will reflect on an extraordinary, undeniable fact: Over time, free nations grow stronger and dictatorships grow weaker. In the middle of the 20th century, some imagined that the central planning and social regimentation were a shortcut to national strength. In fact, the prosperity, and social vitality and technological progress of a people are directly determined by extent of their liberty. Freedom honors and unleashes human creativity -- and creativity determines the strength and wealth of nations. Liberty is both the plan of Heaven for humanity, and the best hope for progress here on Earth.

The progress of liberty is a powerful trend. Yet, we also know that liberty, if not defended, can be lost. The success of freedom is not determined by some dialectic of history. By definition, the success of freedom rests upon the choices and the courage of free peoples, and upon their willingness to sacrifice. In the trenches of World War I, through a two-front war in the 1940s, the difficult battles of Korea and Vietnam, and in missions of rescue and liberation on nearly every continent, Americans have amply displayed our willingness to sacrifice for liberty.

The sacrifices of Americans have not always been recognized or appreciated, yet they have been worthwhile. Because we and our allies were steadfast, Germany and Japan are democratic nations that no longer threaten the world. A global nuclear standoff with the Soviet Union ended peacefully -- as did the Soviet Union. The nations of Europe are moving towards unity, not dividing into armed camps and descending into genocide. Every nation has learned, or should have learned, an important lesson: Freedom is worth fighting for, dying for, and standing for -- and the advance of freedom leads to peace. (Applause.)

And now we must apply that lesson in our own time. We've reached another great turning point -- and the resolve we show will shape the next stage of the world democratic movement.

Our commitment to democracy is tested in countries like Cuba and Burma and North Korea and Zimbabwe -- outposts of oppression in our world. The people in these nations live in captivity, and fear and silence. Yet, these regimes cannot hold back freedom forever -- and, one day, from prison camps and prison cells, and from exile, the leaders of new democracies will arrive. (Applause.) Communism, and militarism and rule by the capricious and corrupt are the relics of a passing era. And we will stand with these oppressed peoples until the day of their freedom finally arrives. (Applause.)

Our commitment to democracy is tested in China. That nation now has a sliver, a fragment of liberty. Yet, China's people will eventually want their liberty pure and whole. China has discovered that economic freedom leads to national wealth. China's leaders will also discover that freedom is indivisible -- that social and religious freedom is also essential to national greatness and national dignity. Eventually, men and women who are allowed to control their own wealth will insist on controlling their own lives and their own country.

Our commitment to democracy is also tested in the Middle East, which is my focus today, and must be a focus of American policy for decades to come. In many nations of the Middle East -- countries of great strategic importance -- democracy has not yet taken root. And the questions arise: Are the peoples of the Middle East somehow beyond the reach of liberty? Are millions of men and women and children condemned by history or culture to live in despotism? Are they alone never to know freedom, and never even to have a choice in the matter? I, for one, do not believe it. I believe every person has the ability and the right to be free. (Applause.)

Some skeptics of democracy assert that the traditions of Islam are inhospitable to the representative government. This "cultural condescension," as Ronald Reagan termed it, has a long history. After the Japanese surrender in 1945, a so-called Japan expert asserted that democracy in that former empire would "never work." Another observer declared the prospects for democracy in post-Hitler Germany are, and I quote, "most uncertain at best" -- he made that claim in 1957. Seventy-four years ago, The Sunday London Times declared nine-tenths of the population of India to be "illiterates not caring a fig for politics." Yet when Indian democracy was imperiled in the 1970s, the Indian people showed their commitment to liberty in a national referendum that saved their form of government.

Time after time, observers have questioned whether this country, or that people, or this group, are "ready" for democracy -- as if freedom were a prize you win for meeting our own Western standards of progress. In fact, the daily work of democracy itself is the path of progress. It teaches cooperation, the free exchange of ideas, and the peaceful resolution of differences. As men and women are showing, from Bangladesh to Botswana, to Mongolia, it is the practice of democracy that makes a nation ready for democracy, and every nation can start on this path.

It should be clear to all that Islam -- the faith of one-fifth of humanity -- is consistent with democratic rule. Democratic progress is found in many predominantly Muslim countries -- in Turkey and Indonesia, and Senegal and Albania, Niger and Sierra Leone. Muslim men and women are good citizens of India and South Africa, of the nations of Western Europe, and of the United States of America.

More than half of all the Muslims in the world live in freedom under democratically constituted governments. They succeed in democratic societies, not in spite of their faith, but because of it. A religion that demands individual moral accountability, and encourages the encounter of the individual with God, is fully compatible with the rights and responsibilities of self-government.

Yet there's a great challenge today in the Middle East. In the words of a recent report by Arab scholars, the global wave of democracy has -- and I quote -- "barely reached the Arab states." They continue: "This freedom deficit undermines human development and is one of the most painful manifestations of lagging political development." The freedom deficit they describe has terrible consequences, of the people of the Middle East and for the world. In many Middle Eastern countries, poverty is deep and it is spreading, women lack rights and are denied schooling. Whole societies remain stagnant while the world moves ahead. These are not the failures of a culture or a religion. These are the failures of political and economic doctrines.

As the colonial era passed away, the Middle East saw the establishment of many military dictatorships. Some rulers adopted the dogmas of socialism, seized total control of political parties and the media and universities. They allied themselves with the Soviet bloc and with international terrorism. Dictators in Iraq and Syria promised the restoration of national honor, a return to ancient glories. They've left instead a legacy of torture, oppression, misery, and ruin.

Other men, and groups of men, have gained influence in the Middle East and beyond through an ideology of theocratic terror. Behind their language of religion is the ambition for absolute political power. Ruling cabals like the

Taliban show their version of religious piety in public whippings of women, ruthless suppression of any difference or dissent, and support for terrorists who arm and train to murder the innocent. The Taliban promised religious purity and national pride. Instead, by systematically destroying a proud and working society, they left behind suffering and starvation.

Many Middle Eastern governments now understand that military dictatorship and theocratic rule are a straight, smooth highway to nowhere. But some governments still cling to the old habits of central control. There are governments that still fear and repress independent thought and creativity, and private enterprise -- the human qualities that make for a -- strong and successful societies. Even when these nations have vast natural resources, they do not respect or develop their greatest resources -- the talent and energy of men and women working and living in freedom.

Instead of dwelling on past wrongs and blaming others, governments in the Middle East need to confront real problems, and serve the true interests of their nations. The good and capable people of the Middle East all deserve responsible leadership. For too long, many people in that region have been victims and subjects -- they deserve to be active citizens.

Governments across the Middle East and North Africa are beginning to see the need for change. Morocco has a diverse new parliament; King Mohammed has urged it to extend the rights to women. Here is how His Majesty explained his reforms to parliament: "How can society achieve progress while women, who represent half the nation, see their rights violated and suffer as a result of injustice, violence, and marginalization, notwithstanding the dignity and justice granted to them by our glorious religion?" The King of Morocco is correct: The future of Muslim nations will be better for all with the full participation of women. (Applause.)

In Bahrain last year, citizens elected their own parliament for the first time in nearly three decades. Oman has extended the vote to all adult citizens; Qatar has a new constitution; Yemen has a multiparty political system; Kuwait has a directly elected national assembly; and Jordan held historic elections this summer. Recent surveys in Arab nations reveal broad support for political pluralism, the rule of law, and free speech. These are the stirrings of Middle Eastern democracy, and they carry the promise of greater change to come.

As changes come to the Middle Eastern region, those with power should ask themselves: Will they be remembered for resisting reform, or for leading it? In Iran, the demand for democracy is strong and broad, as we saw last month when thousands gathered to welcome home Shirin Ebadi, the winner of the Nobel Peace Prize. The regime in Teheran must heed the democratic demands of the Iranian people, or lose its last claim to legitimacy. (Applause.)

For the Palestinian people, the only path to independence and dignity and progress is the path of democracy. (Applause.) And the Palestinian leaders who block and undermine democratic reform, and feed hatred and encourage violence are not leaders at all. They're the main obstacles to peace, and to the success of the Palestinian people.

The Saudi government is taking first steps toward reform, including a plan for gradual introduction of elections. By giving the Saudi people a greater role in their own society, the Saudi government can demonstrate true leadership in the region.

The great and proud nation of Egypt has shown the way toward peace in the Middle East, and now should show the way toward democracy in the Middle East. (Applause.) Champions of democracy in the region understand that democracy is not perfect, it is not the path to utopia, but it's the only path to national success and dignity.

As we watch and encourage reforms in the region, we are mindful that modernization is not the same as Westernization. Representative governments in the Middle East will reflect their own cultures. They will not, and should not, look like us. Democratic nations may be constitutional monarchies, federal republics, or parliamentary systems. And working democracies always need time to develop -- as did our own. We've taken a 200-year journey toward inclusion and justice -- and this makes us patient and understanding as other nations are at different stages of this journey.

There are, however, essential principles common to every successful society, in every culture. Successful societies limit the power of the state and the power of the military -- so that governments respond to the will of the people, and not the will of an elite. Successful societies protect freedom with the consistent and impartial rule of law, instead of selecting applying -- selectively applying the law to punish political opponents. Successful societies allow room for healthy civic institutions -- for political parties and labor unions and independent newspapers and broadcast media. Successful societies guarantee religious liberty -- the right to serve and honor God without fear of persecution. Successful societies privatize their economies, and secure the rights of property. They prohibit and punish official corruption, and invest in the health and education of their people. They recognize the rights of women. And instead of directing hatred and resentment against others, successful societies appeal to the hopes of their own people. (Applause.)

These vital principles are being applies in the nations of Afghanistan and Iraq. With the steady leadership of President Karzai, the people of Afghanistan are building a modern and peaceful government. Next month, 500 delegates will convene a national assembly in Kabul to approve a new Afghan constitution. The proposed draft would establish a bicameral parliament, set national elections next year, and recognize Afghanistan's Muslim identity, while protecting the rights of all citizens. Afghanistan faces continuing economic and security challenges -- it will face those challenges as a free and stable democracy. (Applause.)

In Iraq, the Coalition Provisional Authority and the Iraqi Governing Council are also working together to build a democracy -- and after three decades of tyranny, this work is not easy. The former dictator ruled by terror and treachery, and left deeply ingrained habits of fear and distrust. Remnants of his regime, joined by foreign terrorists, continue their battle against order and against civilization. Our coalition is responding to recent attacks with precision raids, guided by intelligence provided by the Iraqis, themselves. And we're working closely with Iraqi citizens as they prepare a constitution, as they move toward free elections and take increasing responsibility for their own affairs. As in the defense of Greece in 1947, and later in the Berlin Airlift, the strength and will of free peoples are now being tested before a watching world. And we will meet this test. (Applause.)

Securing democracy in Iraq is the work of many hands. American and coalition forces are sacrificing for the peace of Iraq and for the security of free nations. Aid workers from many countries are facing danger to help the Iraqi people. The National Endowment for Democracy is promoting women's rights, and training Iraqi journalists, and teaching the skills of political participation. Iraqis, themselves -- police and borders guards and local officials -- are joining in the work and they are sharing in the sacrifice.

This is a massive and difficult undertaking -- it is worth our effort, it is worth our sacrifice, because we know the stakes. The failure of Iraqi democracy would embolden terrorists around the world, increase dangers to the American people, and extinguish the hopes of millions in the region. Iraqi democracy will succeed -- and that success will send forth the news, from Damascus to Teheran -- that freedom can be the future of every nation. (Applause.) The establishment of a free Iraq at the heart of the Middle East will be a watershed event in the global democratic revolution. (Applause.)

Sixty years of Western nations excusing and accommodating the lack of freedom in the Middle East did nothing to make us safe -- because in the long run, stability cannot be purchased at the expense of liberty. As long as the Middle East remains a place where freedom does not flourish, it will remain a place of stagnation, resentment, and violence ready for export. And with the spread of weapons that can bring catastrophic harm to our country and to our friends, it would be reckless to accept the status quo. (Applause.)

Therefore, the United States has adopted a new policy, a forward strategy of freedom in the Middle East. This strategy requires the same persistence and energy and idealism we have shown before. And it will yield the same results. As in Europe, as in Asia, as in every region of the world, the advance of freedom leads to peace. (Applause.)

The advance of freedom is the calling of our time; it is the calling of our country. From the Fourteen Points to the Four Freedoms, to the Speech at Westminster, America has put our power at the service of principle. We believe that liberty is the design of nature; we believe that liberty is the direction of history. We believe that human fulfillment and excellence come in the responsible exercise of liberty. And we believe that freedom -- the freedom we prize -- is not for us alone, it is the right and the capacity of all mankind. (Applause.)

Working for the spread of freedom can be hard. Yet, America has accomplished hard tasks before. Our nation is strong; we're strong of heart. And we're not alone. Freedom is finding allies in every country; freedom finds allies in every culture. And as we meet the terror and violence of the world, we can be certain the author of freedom is not indifferent to the fate of freedom.

With all the tests and all the challenges of our age, this is, above all, the age of liberty. Each of you at this Endowment is fully engaged in the great cause of liberty. And I thank you. May God bless your work. And may God continue to bless America. (Applause.)

END 11:37 A.M. EST

President Bush's Inaugural Address 2005

Vice President Cheney, Mr. Chief Justice, President Carter, President Bush, President Clinton, reverend clergy, distinguished guests, fellow citizens:

On this day, prescribed by law and marked by ceremony, we celebrate the durable wisdom of our Constitution, and recall the deep commitments that unite our country. I am grateful for the honor of this hour, mindful of the consequential times in which we live, and determined to fulfill the oath that I have sworn and you have witnessed.

At this second gathering, our duties are defined not by the words I use, but by the history we have seen together. For a half century, America defended our own freedom by standing watch on distant borders. After the shipwreck of communism came years of relative quiet, years of repose, years of sabbatical - and then there came a day of fire.

We have seen our vulnerability - and we have seen its deepest source. For as long as whole regions of the world simmer in resentment and tyranny - prone to ideologies that feed hatred and excuse murder - violence will gather, and multiply in destructive power, and cross the most defended borders, and raise a mortal threat. There is only one force of history that can break the reign of hatred and resentment, and expose the pretensions of tyrants, and reward the hopes of the decent and tolerant, and that is the force of human freedom.

We are led, by events and common sense, to one conclusion: The survival of liberty in our land increasingly depends on the success of liberty in other lands. The best hope for peace in our world is the expansion of freedom in all the world.

America's vital interests and our deepest beliefs are now one. From the day of our Founding, we have proclaimed that every man and woman on this earth has rights, and dignity, and matchless value, because they bear the image of the Maker of Heaven and earth. Across the generations we have proclaimed the imperative of self-government, because no one is fit to be a master, and no one deserves to be a slave. Advancing these ideals is the mission that created our Nation. It is the honorable achievement of our fathers. Now it is the urgent requirement of our nation's security, and the calling of our time.

So it is the policy of the United States to seek and support the growth of democratic movements and institutions in every nation and culture, with the ultimate goal of ending tyranny in our world.

This is not primarily the task of arms, though we will defend ourselves and our friends by force of arms when necessary. Freedom, by its nature, must be chosen, and defended by citizens, and sustained by the rule of law and the protection of minorities. And when the soul of a nation finally speaks, the institutions that arise may reflect customs and traditions very different from our own. America will not impose our own style of government on the unwilling. Our goal instead is to help others find their own voice, attain their own freedom, and make their own way.

The great objective of ending tyranny is the concentrated work of generations. The difficulty of the task is no excuse for avoiding it. America's influence is not unlimited, but fortunately for the oppressed, America's influence is considerable, and we will use it confidently in freedom's cause.

My most solemn duty is to protect this nation and its people against further attacks and emerging threats. Some have unwisely chosen to test America's resolve, and have found it firm.

We will persistently clarify the choice before every ruler and every nation: The moral choice between oppression, which is always wrong, and freedom, which is eternally right. America will not pretend that jailed dissidents prefer their chains, or that women welcome humiliation and servitude, or that any human being aspires to live at the mercy of bullies.

We will encourage reform in other governments by making clear that success in our relations will require the decent treatment of their own people. America's belief in human dignity will guide our policies, yet rights must be more than the grudging concessions of dictators; they are secured by free dissent and the participation of the governed. In the long run, there is no justice without freedom, and there can be no human rights without human liberty.

Some, I know, have questioned the global appeal of liberty - though this time in history, four decades defined by the swiftest advance of freedom ever seen, is an odd time for doubt. Americans, of all people, should never be surprised by the power of our ideals. Eventually, the call of freedom comes to every mind and every soul. We do not accept the existence of permanent tyranny because we do not accept the possibility of permanent slavery. Liberty will come to those who love it.

Today, America speaks anew to the peoples of the world:

All who live in tyranny and hopelessness can know: the United States will not ignore your oppression, or excuse your oppressors. When you stand for your liberty, we will stand with you.

Democratic reformers facing repression, prison, or exile can know: America sees you for who you are: the future leaders of your free country.

The rulers of outlaw regimes can know that we still believe as Abraham Lincoln did: "Those who deny freedom to others deserve it not for themselves; and, under the rule of a just God, cannot long retain it."

The leaders of governments with long habits of control need to know: To serve your people you must learn to trust them. Start on this journey of progress and justice, and America will walk at your side.

And all the allies of the United States can know: we honor your friendship, we rely on your counsel, and we depend on your help. Division among free nations is a primary goal of freedom's enemies. The concerted effort of free nations to promote democracy is a prelude to our enemies' defeat.

Today, I also speak anew to my fellow citizens:

From all of you, I have asked patience in the hard task of securing America, which you have granted in good measure. Our country has accepted obligations that are difficult to fulfill, and would be dishonorable to abandon. Yet because we have acted in the great liberating tradition of this nation, tens of millions have achieved their freedom. And as hope kindles hope, millions more will find it. By our efforts, we have lit a fire as well - a fire in the minds of men. It warms those who feel its power, it burns those who fight its progress, and one day this untamed fire of freedom will reach the darkest corners of our world.

A few Americans have accepted the hardest duties in this cause - in the quiet work of intelligence and diplomacy ... the idealistic work of helping raise up free governments ... the dangerous and necessary work of fighting our enemies. Some have shown their devotion to our country in deaths that honored their whole lives - and we will always honor their names and their sacrifice.

All Americans have witnessed this idealism, and some for the first time. I ask our youngest citizens to believe the evidence of your eyes. You have seen duty and allegiance in the determined faces of our soldiers. You have seen that life is fragile, and evil is real, and courage triumphs. Make the choice to serve in a cause larger than your wants, larger than yourself - and in your days you will add not just to the wealth of our country, but to its character.

America has need of idealism and courage, because we have essential work at home - the unfinished work of American freedom. In a world moving toward liberty, we are determined to show the meaning and promise of liberty.

In America's ideal of freedom, citizens find the dignity and security of economic independence, instead of laboring on the edge of subsistence. This is the broader definition of liberty that motivated the Homestead Act, the Social Security Act, and the G.I. Bill of Rights. And now we will extend this vision by reforming great institutions to serve the needs of our time. To give every American a stake in the promise and future of our country, we will bring the highest standards to our schools, and build an ownership society. We will widen the ownership of homes and businesses, retirement savings and health insurance - preparing our people for the challenges of life in a free society. By making every citizen an agent of his or her own destiny, we will give our fellow Americans greater freedom from want and fear, and make our society more prosperous and just and equal.

In America's ideal of freedom, the public interest depends on private character - on integrity, and tolerance toward others, and the rule of conscience in our own lives. Self-government relies, in the end, on the governing of the self. That edifice of character is built in families, supported by communities with standards, and sustained in our national life by the truths of Sinai, the Sermon on the Mount, the words of the Koran, and the varied faiths of our people. Americans move forward in every generation by reaffirming all that is good and true that came before - ideals of justice and conduct that are the same yesterday, today, and forever.

In America's ideal of freedom, the exercise of rights is ennobled by service, and mercy, and a heart for the weak. Liberty for all does not mean independence from one another. Our nation relies on men and women who look after a neighbor and surround the lost with love. Americans, at our best, value the life we see in one another, and must always remember that even the unwanted have worth. And our country must abandon all the habits of racism, because we cannot carry the message of freedom and the baggage of bigotry at the same time.

From the perspective of a single day, including this day of dedication, the issues and questions before our country are many. From the viewpoint of centuries, the questions that come to us are narrowed and few. Did our generation advance the cause of freedom? And did our character bring credit to that cause?

These questions that judge us also unite us, because Americans of every party and background, Americans by choice and by birth, are bound to one another in the cause of freedom. We have known divisions, which must be healed to move forward in great purposes - and I will strive in good faith to heal them. Yet those divisions do not define America. We felt the unity and fellowship of our nation when freedom came under attack, and our response came like a single hand over a single heart. And we can feel that same unity and pride whenever America acts for good, and the victims of disaster are given hope, and the unjust encounter justice, and the captives are set free.

We go forward with complete confidence in the eventual triumph of freedom. Not because history runs on the wheels of inevitability; it is human choices that move events. Not because we consider ourselves a chosen nation; God moves and chooses as He wills. We have confidence because freedom is the permanent hope of mankind, the hunger in dark places, the longing of the soul. When our Founders declared a new order of the ages; when soldiers died in wave upon wave for a union based on liberty; when citizens marched in peaceful outrage under the banner "Freedom Now" - they were acting on an ancient hope that is meant to be fulfilled. History has an ebb and flow of justice, but history also has a visible direction, set by liberty and the Author of Liberty.

When the Declaration of Independence was first read in public and the Liberty Bell was sounded in celebration, a witness said, "It rang as if it meant something." In our time it means something still. America, in this young century, proclaims liberty throughout all the world, and to all the inhabitants thereof. Renewed in our strength - tested, but not weary - we are ready for the greatest achievements in the history of freedom.

May God bless you, and may He watch over the United States of America.

President's Address to the Nation
The Oval Office

December 18, 2005

9:01 P.M. EST

THE PRESIDENT: Good evening. Three days ago, in large numbers, Iraqis went to the polls to choose their own leaders -- a landmark day in the history of liberty. In the coming weeks, the ballots will be counted, a new government formed, and a people who suffered in tyranny for so long will become full members of the free world.

This election will not mean the end of violence. But it is the beginning of something new: constitutional democracy at the heart of the Middle East. And this vote -- 6,000 miles away, in a vital region of the world -- means that America has an ally of growing strength in the fight against terror.

All who had a part in this achievement -- Iraqis, and Americans and our coalition partners -- can be proud. Yet our work is not done. There is more testing and sacrifice before us. I know many Americans have questions about the cost and direction of this war. So tonight I want to talk to you about how far we have come in Iraq, and the path that lies ahead.

From this office, nearly three years ago, I announced the start of military operations in Iraq. Our coalition confronted a regime that defied United Nations Security Council resolutions, violated a cease-fire agreement, sponsored terrorism, and possessed, we believed, weapons of mass destruction. After the swift fall of Baghdad, we found mass graves filled by a dictator; we found some capacity to restart programs to produce weapons of mass destruction, but we did not find those weapons.

It is true that Saddam Hussein had a history of pursuing and using weapons of mass destruction. It is true that he systematically concealed those programs, and blocked the work of U.N. weapons inspectors. It is true that many nations believed that Saddam had weapons of mass destruction. But much of the intelligence turned out to be wrong. As your President, I am responsible for the decision to go into Iraq. Yet it was right to remove Saddam Hussein from power.

He was given an ultimatum -- and he made his choice for war. And the result of that war was to rid a -- the world of a murderous dictator who menaced his people, invaded his neighbors, and declared America to be his enemy. Saddam Hussein, captured and jailed, is still the same raging tyrant -- only now without a throne. His power to harm a single man, woman, or child is gone forever. And the world is better for it.

Since the removal of Saddam, this war, like other wars in our history, has been difficult. The mission of American troops in urban raids and desert patrols, fighting Saddam loyalists and foreign terrorists, has brought danger and suffering and loss. This loss has caused sorrow for our whole nation -- and it has led some to ask if we are creating more problems than we're solving.

That is an important question, and the answer depends on your view of the war on terror. If you think the terrorists would become peaceful if only America would stop provoking them, then it might make sense to leave them alone.

This is not the threat I see. I see a global terrorist movement that exploits Islam in the service of radical political aims -- a vision in which books are burned, and women are oppressed, and all dissent is crushed. Terrorist operatives conduct their campaign of murder with a set of declared and specific goals -- to de-moralize free nations, to drive us out of the Middle East, to spread an empire of fear across that region, and to wage a perpetual war against America and our friends. These terrorists view the world as a giant battlefield -- and they seek to attack us wherever they can. This has attracted al Qaeda to Iraq, where they are attempting to frighten and intimidate America into a policy of retreat.

The terrorists do not merely object to American actions in Iraq and elsewhere, they object to our deepest values and our way of life. And if we were not fighting them in Iraq, in Afghanistan, in Southeast Asia, and in other places, the terrorists would not be peaceful citizens, they would be on the offense, and headed our way.

September the 11th, 2001 required us to take every emerging threat to our country seriously, and it shattered the illusion that terrorists attack us only after we provoke them. On that day, we were not in Iraq, we were not in Afghanistan, but the terrorists attacked us anyway -- and killed nearly 3,000 men, women, and children in our own country. My conviction comes down to this: We do not create terrorism by fighting the terrorists. We invite terrorism by ignoring them. And we will defeat the terrorists by capturing and killing them abroad, removing their safe havens, and strengthening new allies like Iraq and Afghanistan in the fight we share.

The work in Iraq has been especially difficult -- more difficult than we expected. Reconstruction efforts and the training of Iraqi security forces started more slowly than we hoped. We continue to see violence and suffering, caused by an enemy that is determined and brutal, unconstrained by conscience or the rules of war.

Some look at the challenges in Iraq and conclude that the war is lost, and not worth another dime or another day. I don't believe that. Our military commanders do not believe that. Our troops in the field, who bear the burden and make the sacrifice, do not believe that America has lost. And not even the terrorists believe it. We know from their own communications that they feel a tightening noose, and fear the rise of a democratic Iraq.

The terrorists will continue to have the coward's power to plant roadside bombs and recruit suicide bombers. And you will continue to see the grim results on the evening news. This proves that the war is difficult -- it doesn't mean that we are losing. Behind the images of chaos that terrorists create for the cameras, we are making steady gains with a clear objective in view.

America, our coalition, and Iraqi leaders are working toward the same goal -- a democratic Iraq that can defend itself, that will never again be a safe haven for terrorists, and that will serve as a model of freedom for the Middle East.

We have put in place a strategy to achieve this goal -- a strategy I've been discussing in detail over the last few weeks. This plan has three critical elements.

First, our coalition will remain on the offense -- finding and clearing out the enemy, transferring control of more territory to Iraqi units, and building up the Iraqi security forces so they can increasingly lead the fight. At this time last year, there were only a handful of Iraqi army and police battalions ready for combat. Now, there are more than 125 Iraqi combat battalions fighting the enemy, more than 50 are taking the lead, and we have transferred more than a dozen military bases to Iraqi control.

Second, we're helping the Iraqi government establish the institutions of a unified and lasting democracy, in which all of Iraq's people are included and represented. Here also, the news is encouraging. Three days ago, more than 10 million Iraqis went to the polls -- including many Sunni Iraqis who had boycotted national elections last January. Iraqis of every background are recognizing that democracy is the future of the country they love -- and they want their voices heard. One Iraqi, after dipping his finger in the purple ink as he cast his ballot, stuck his finger in the air and said: "This is a thorn in the eyes of the terrorists." Another voter was asked, "Are you Sunni or Shia?" And he responded, "I am Iraqi."

Third, after a number of setbacks, our coalition is moving forward with a reconstruction plan to revive Iraq's economy and infrastructure -- and to give Iraqis confidence that a free life will be a better life. Today in Iraq, seven in 10 Iraqis say their lives are going well, and nearly two-thirds expect things to improve even more in the year ahead. Despite the violence, Iraqis are optimistic -- and that optimism is justified.

In all three aspects of our strategy -- security, democracy, and reconstruction -- we have learned from our experiences, and fixed what has not worked. We will continue to listen to honest criticism, and make every change that will help us complete the mission. Yet there is a difference between honest critics who recognize what is wrong, and defeatists who refuse to see that anything is right.

Defeatism may have its partisan uses, but it is not justified by the facts. For every scene of destruction in Iraq, there are more scenes of rebuilding and hope. For every life lost, there are countless more lives reclaimed. And for every terrorist working to stop freedom in Iraq, there are many more Iraqis and Americans working to defeat them. My fellow citizens: Not only can we win the war in Iraq, we are winning the war in Iraq.

It is also important for every American to understand the consequences of pulling out of Iraq before our work is done. We would abandon our Iraqi friends and signal to the world that America cannot be trusted to keep its word. We would undermine the morale of our troops by betraying the cause for which they have sacrificed. We would cause the tyrants in the Middle East to laugh at our failed resolve, and tighten their repressive grip. We would hand Iraq over to enemies who have pledged to attack us and the global terrorist movement would be emboldened and more dangerous than ever before. To retreat before victory would be an act of recklessness and dishonor, and I will not allow it.

We're approaching a new year, and there are certain things all Americans can expect to see. We will see more sacrifice -- from our military, their families, and the Iraqi people. We will see a concerted effort to improve Iraqi police forces and fight corruption. We will see the Iraqi military gaining strength and confidence, and the democratic process moving forward. As these achievements come, it should require fewer American troops to accomplish our mission. I will make decisions on troop levels based on the progress we see on the ground and the advice of our military leaders -- not based on artificial timetables set by politicians in Washington. Our forces in Iraq are on the road to victory -- and that is the road that will take them home.

In the months ahead, all Americans will have a part in the success of this war. Members of Congress will need to provide resources for our military. Our men and women in uniform, who have done so much already, will continue their brave and urgent work. And tonight, I ask all of you listening to carefully consider the stakes of this war, to realize how far we have come and the good we are doing, and to have patience in this difficult, noble, and necessary cause.

I also want to speak to those of you who did not support my decision to send troops to Iraq: I have heard your disagreement, and I know how deeply it is felt. Yet now there are only two options before our country -- victory or defeat. And the need for victory is larger than any president or political party, because the security of our people is in the balance. I don't expect you to support everything I do, but tonight I have a request: Do not give in to despair, and do not give up on this fight for freedom.

Americans can expect some things of me, as well. My most solemn responsibility is to protect our nation, and that requires me to make some tough decisions. I see the consequences of those decisions when I meet wounded servicemen and women who cannot leave their hospital beds, but summon the strength to look me in the eye and say they would do it all over again. I see the consequences when I talk to parents who miss a child so much -- but tell me he loved being a soldier, he believed in his mission, and, Mr. President, finish the job.

I know that some of my decisions have led to terrible loss -- and not one of those decisions has been taken lightly. I know this war is controversial -- yet being your President requires doing what I believe is right and accepting the consequences. And I have never been more certain that America's actions in Iraq are essential to the security of our citizens, and will lay the foundation of peace for our children and grandchildren.

Next week, Americans will gather to celebrate Christmas and Hanukkah. Many families will be praying for loved ones spending this season far from home -- in Iraq, Afghanistan, and other dangerous places. Our nation joins in those prayers. We pray for the safety and strength of our troops. We trust, with them, in a love that conquers all fear, in a light that reaches the darkest corners of the Earth. And we remember the words of the Christmas carol, written during the Civil War: "God is not dead, nor [does] He sleep; the Wrong shall fail, the Right prevail, with peace on Earth, goodwill to men."

Thank you, and good night.

END 9:18 P.M. EST